S0-ADJ-967

❖ Common Morality

Common Morality ∷ *Deciding What to Do*

B E R N A R D   G E R T

OXFORD
UNIVERSITY PRESS

OXFORD
UNIVERSITY PRESS

Oxford University Press, Inc., publishes works that further
Oxford University's objective of excellence
in research, scholarship, and education.

Oxford   New York
Auckland   Cape Town   Dar es Salaam   Hong Kong   Karachi
Kuala Lumpur   Madrid   Melbourne   Mexico City   Nairobi
New Delhi   Shanghai   Taipei   Toronto

With offices in
Argentina   Austria   Brazil   Chile   Czech Republic   France   Greece
Guatemala   Hungary   Italy   Japan   Poland   Portugal   Singapore
South Korea   Switzerland   Thailand   Turkey   Ukraine   Vietnam

Copyright © 2004 by Oxford University Press, Inc.

Published by Oxford University Press, Inc.
198 Madison Avenue, New York, New York 10016

www.oup.com

First issued as an Oxford University Press paperback, 2007

Oxford is a registered trademark of Oxford University Press

All rights reserved. No part of this publication may be reproduced,
stored in a retrieval system, or transmitted, in any form or by any means,
electronic, mechanical, photocopying, recording, or otherwise,
without the prior permission of Oxford University Press.

Library of Congress Cataloging-in-Publication Data
Gert, Bernard, 1934–
Common morality : deciding what to do / Bernard Gert.
p. cm.
Includes bibliographical references and index.
ISBN-13 978-0-19-517371-0; 978-0-19-531421-2 (pbk)
ISBN 0-19-517371-6; 0-19-531421-2 (pbk)
1. Ethics. 2. Title.

BJ1012.G445 2004
170'.44–dc22   2003066200

1 3 5 7 9 8 6 4 2

Printed in the United States of America
on acid-free paper

❖ Preface

This book provides accounts of impartiality and rationality and shows how they are related to our common morality. Common morality is the moral system that thoughtful people use, usually implicitly, when they make moral decisions and judgments. It is the only guide to behavior affecting others that all rational persons understand and upon which they can all agree. Although this agreement is only an agreement on the general framework with which to consider moral problems, common morality does distinguish between morally acceptable and morally unacceptable solutions. While not providing a unique solution to any genuinely controversial moral issue, it allows for morally acceptable procedures for settling all controversial issues. It also provides moral support for establishing the kinds of democratic governments and political institutions that allow everyone to participate in the decisions that will affect their lives.

Common morality is also the only guide for governing our behavior toward others that is based on nothing other than the universal features of our common human nature such as our fallibility, rationality, and vulnerability. It is not a moral system that is derived from my moral theory. On the contrary, I attempt to provide a clear, coherent, and comprehensive description of common morality before I attempt to show how this moral system can be justified. I recognize and accept that common morality does not provide unique answers to every moral question. I do not try to make morality do more than it can. It would be a mistake to hold that I had invented, or even discovered, any new moral truths. Nothing I say should be surprising in the least. My only claim to originality concerning morality is in the explicitness of my recognition of its limitations.

My justification of morality is similarly modest. My attempt to show that all rational persons would endorse morality is qualified, depending on extreme limitations on the beliefs that can be used as well as other conditions. I do not try to show that it is irrational to act immorally; I show only that it is never irrational to act morally. I am trying to do far less than what philosophers from Plato on have failed to do. Thus, even if I succeed completely in what I am trying to do, people may be disappointed. It is also disappointing that there is no perpetual-motion machine.

My description of morality may not be one that people want to hear. That is unfortunate, because this description of morality provides the kind of moral framework that can be accepted by all rational persons. It can help people make better moral decisions and judgments in difficult cases by clarifying the kind of action involved. It allows people with different views on what morally ought to be done to talk to one another and see that their disagreements occur within a much larger area of agreement. It may persuade people to accept that those who disagree with them may be holding morally acceptable views. It promotes fruitful and respectful conversation. It eliminates both dogmatism and relativism. It does everything that people can reasonably expect a description of morality to do.

Common morality does not provide the kind of simple procedure for deciding what morally ought to be done that most philosophers claim to provide. It sets limits on what is morally acceptable, but it rarely provides a unique solution to a morally controversial problem. Although common morality applies to all rational persons, rational people need not act morally, and if they are in a privileged position, they need not even endorse acting morally. Nonetheless, with appropriate qualifications, rationality does support morality.

People need such a detailed description of morality only because their natural understanding of morality has been distorted by slogans, both philosophical and religious, such as the Golden Rule, the Ten Commandments, and Kant's Categorical Imperative.[1] Not surprisingly, people prefer descriptions of morality that provide simple procedures for determining what they morally ought to do. Kant's Categorical Imperative and Mill's Principle of Utility are two such seemingly simple procedures.[2] Even though none of these procedures are adequate to determine what morally ought to be done in all cases, they are so attractive that many have tried to revise and repair them, or to provide new procedures that will give a unique answer to every moral question. They have not done so and cannot do so, because there is not a unique answer to every moral question, and hence there cannot be any procedure that settles every moral issue.

The way that ethics is taught, especially in introductory courses and in courses in applied ethics, is a matter of serious concern. In these courses, it is standard practice to present moral theories such as those in Mill's *Utilitarianism* and Kant's *Groundwork* or some textbook variation of these as if they were adequate. Although all philosophers recognize that all of the standard theories, including those by Kant and Mill, are inadequate, they still often put them forward as if students should choose between them. Even worse, students are sometimes told that they should choose the theory that seems to work best for the particular problem with which they are concerned. This results in students being Kantians or Utilitarians depending on the problem they are considering, which is a trivialization not only of these theories but of moral theories in general.

Philosophers put forward moral theories in order to provide clear, coherent, and comprehensive descriptions of morality and its justification. No philosopher would accept the view that his theory provides incorrect answers to some moral questions, even if it is granted that it provides correct answers to most others. Almost all moral theories, on the standard interpretations, provide correct answers to most noncontroversial moral questions. However, if a moral theory gives an incorrect answer to any noncontroversial moral question, it cannot be trusted to give a correct answer to any controversial moral question. To claim that a moral theory gives an incorrect answer to any moral problem is to reject that theory or, at least, to require that it be revised.

The moral theories put forward by Kant and Mill do give incorrect answers to some moral questions. Of course, theories can be revised and there are now many variations of the theories of Kant and Mill, but none of them is without significant flaws. Many presuppose that there is a decision procedure that provides a unique correct solution to every moral problem. However, it is an important feature of common morality that there is not a unique correct answer to every moral question. A moral theory must not only explain and justify the overwhelming agreement on most moral issues but also explain and justify the significant disagreement on controversial moral issues.

Common morality is the foundation for all philosophical theories of morality. All of these theories, even those that allow for some revision of morality, incorporate what they take to be its essential elements. Kant incorporates the feature that morality requires impartiality. Mill incorporates the feature that morality is concerned with the consequences of actions. Negative consequentialists incorporate the feature that morality is more concerned with lessening harm than with promoting good. Social-contract theorists incorporate the feature that morality must be acceptable to all rational agents. Natural-law theorists incorporate the feature that morality must be known to all normal adult human beings. I incorporate all of these features of common morality in my theory, so it is not surprising that it resembles all of these other standard moral theories in some respects. However, my account of morality and its justification contains features that are not found together in any of the traditional theories, so the reader should be wary of classifying it as a version of any of the traditional moral theories.

This book is the result of almost forty years of work. In 1966 I finished the first complete draft of the moral theory that, with revisions, this book presents. In 1970 *The Moral Rules: A New Rational Foundation for Morality* was published by Harper and Row. I chose a trade publisher rather than an academic press because I thought that I had written a book that would be of interest to the general public. Two slight revisions of that book appeared as Harper Torchbooks in 1973 and 1975, and a German translation of the book was published in 1983. Although the book remained in print, it did not have sufficient sales for Harper and Row to agree to publish my extensive revision of the theory. However, thanks to a review by Kurt Baier, Oxford University Press published the revised and enlarged version in 1988 under the title *Morality: A New Justification of the Moral Rules*. They issued another extensively revised and enlarged version in 1998 under the title *Morality: Its Nature and Justification*. *Common Morality* is the first version of my theory that is shorter than all these previous versions.

Detailed discussions of all the points presented in this book are offered in the revised edition of *Morality: Its Nature and Justification*. As pointed out in the Acknowledgements, due to several symposia on the original edition of that book, this book contains some revisions of the views presented there. I am grateful to Oxford University Press for agreeing to publish a revision of that book, so that readers who are not completely persuaded by this book can consult that larger work to find detailed arguments, all of which are consistent with the views presented in this book. It is still extremely unlikely that there are no remaining unclarities or even mistakes in this presentation of common morality; nevertheless, I am confident that my description of our common morality provides a close approximation to it. Similarly, although there may be mistakes in my justification of the moral system, I am confident that I have justified it in as strong a way as it is possible to do without distorting the concepts involved.

That, after forty years, I am still trying to describe and justify morality in a way that will be of interest to the general public as well as to philosophers is another example of the triumph of hope over experience. However, that there is even a small chance that this book may help make people aware that they share a common morality and that all of their moral disagreements occur within a larger area of moral agreement makes it worth the effort. Now that people with the most diverse cultural and religious views must interact with each other, it is important for everyone to be aware of their common morality. It is especially important for people to distinguish morality from religion and to realize that they should not follow the dictates of their religion when these conflict with morality. I am aware—indeed, it is a significant feature of my description of morality—that rational persons need not accept morality as their overriding guide to conduct. However, we now know how much death and destruction arise from allowing any other guide—personal, national, racial, or religious—to overrule the moral guide. Universal acceptance that no other guide can overrule common morality may now be the only way that we can avoid complete disaster.

⠶ Acknowledgments

I am grateful to Dartmouth College, where I have been teaching for over forty years, for providing me with the perfect environment for writing and teaching. I developed and improved my moral theory by teaching it to many generations of challenging Dartmouth students. This version of my theory directly benefited by being used in a Junior Honors seminar with six Dartmouth students on a Foreign Study Program at the University of Edinburgh in the fall term of 2002.

A National Endowment for the Humanities Fellowship for the 1969–70 academic year allowed me to finish the first version of my moral theory, *The Moral Rules: A New Rational Foundation for Morality* (New York: Harper and Row, 1970). Due to the efforts of Gregory Prince, then a dean at Dartmouth, now president of Hampshire College, I applied for and was awarded a National Endowment for the Humanities—National Science Foundation Sustained Development Award (1980–84), which enabled me to test my theory by teaching in all of Dartmouth's professional schools, the medical school, the Tuck School of Business, and the Thayer School of Engineering. This resulted in an extensive revision to my theory, which was published as *Morality: A New Justification of the Moral Rules* (Oxford: Oxford University Press, 1988).

More recently, from 1992 to 1998, I was appointed the Eunice and Julian Cohen Professor for the Study of Ethics and Human Values, which, by reducing my teaching load to only two courses a year, enabled me to finish several books, including another extensive revision, *Morality: Its Nature and Justification* (Oxford: Oxford University Press, 1998). I am extremely grateful to Eunice and Julian Cohen, who endowed that chair.

Most recently, for the academic year 2001–2, I received The Frank H. Kenan Fellowship, permanently endowed by the William Rand Kenan, Jr., Charitable Trust, from the National Humanities Center in North Carolina. This fellowship provided me with an environment that made it almost impossible not to finish this book. Although finishing this book was not one of the projects that I expected to be working on, the terrorist attacks of September 11, 2001, made it seem a more urgent task than my other projects.

I have been very fortunate to have colleagues who took an interest in my work and provided me with significant criticisms and encouragement. Timothy Duggan, who died in 1990, was my best friend and colleague for thirty years. I benefited from discussions with him on every philosophical topic. Larry Stern was the colleague who was most helpful when I was working on the first version of my theory, *The Moral Rules*. Walter Sinnott-Armstrong is the colleague who has been most helpful with all of the subsequent versions, including this one. Walter not only led me to make my points clearer but encouraged me to write these books by offering to use drafts of them in his classes. His comments on what I took to be the final draft of this book resulted in many improvements in organization, style, and substance.

In May 1999, Walter, together with Robert Audi, arranged a wonderful four-day conference on *Morality: Its Nature and Justification*, in which thirteen excellent philosophers, including Walter and Robert, presented papers on that book. The papers at this conference (plus two others) provided me with the opportunity to clarify and modify some of my positions. These clarifications and modifications are made explicit in a book, *Rationality, Rules, and*

Ideals: Critical Essays on Bernard Gert's Moral Theory, edited by
Walter Sinnott-Armstrong and Robert Audi (Rowman and Lit-
tlefield, 2002), which contains a précis of *Morality: Its Nature and
Justification*, the conference papers, and my replies to them.

All of the papers had a significant influence on the account of
morality and its justification offered in the present book. The papers by Walter and Robert were among the most helpful, and each
led to several improvements in the presentation of my theory. Ernst
Tugendhat's remarks persuaded me to emphasize the motivation
provided by my justification of morality. Matthias Kettner showed
me the importance of explaining how the moral system can have
practical value. Geoffrey Sayre-McCord made clear to me how
important it is to include content in the definition of morality.
David Copp's criticisms at the conference and in the *Philosophy and
Phenomenological Review (PPR)* symposium (vol. 62, no. 2, March
2001, pp. 421–81) led me to make explicit and clarify the distinction
between the objective and the personal sense of rationality. Michael
Smith's arguments persuaded me that when concerned with the
objective sense of rationality, it was preferable to regard reasons as
facts rather than as beliefs. His arguments reinforced the point
made by Ted Bond in his review of my book in *Metaphilosophy* 31,
no. 4 (July 2000) and by my son, Joshua in his continuing critiques
of my account of rationality. Shelly Kagan's objections reinforced
the objections made by Dan Brock in the *PPR* symposium and led
me to realize that I had made a mistake in limiting the duty to aid in
special circumstances to civilized societies. Brock also showed me
that the distinction between promoting goods and preventing evils
was less clear-cut than I had thought.

John Deigh helped me to formulate more clearly the distinction
between moral rules and moral ideals. Ted Bond led me to make
an important distinction between moral and social virtues. Susan
Wolf encouraged me by supporting the importance of the moral

rules. Doug MacLean showed me that I needed to be clearer about the goodness of pleasure and the badness of pain, a point that was also forcefully made by Patrick Yarnell in a symposium paper published in the *Journal of Value Inquiry (JVI)* 35, no. 4 (December 2001: 449–54). Because of Frances Kamm I came to see that recognizing that morality is a public system has even more consequences than I had realized. Julia Driver reinforced my view about the seriousness of the problems that arise if moral evaluation is regarded as distinct from the public guide provided by morality. Marcia Baron showed me that I had to be clearer about morality being primarily concerned with the way people behave toward one another.

The other contributors to the *PPR* symposium were also helpful. Kurt Baier, who has influenced me more than any other contemporary philosopher, made me realize the pull of the view that rationality supports acting morally. Thomas Carson made me realize the importance of distinguishing morality from religion. My former student Ruth Chang made it clear why it is so important to take irrationality rather than rationality as the basic concept. The other contributors to the *JVI* symposium were also helpful. David Phillips showed me the importance of clarity about impartiality, and James Sterba, with whom I have had many philosophical exchanges, showed me the importance of clarity about rationality. The generally favorable reception of *Morality: Its Nature and Justification* by the participants at the conference and by the contributors to the *PPR* and *JVI* symposiums and my ability to clarify and modify views to meet their objections were major factors in my decision to write this shorter version of my theory.

Another important factor in my decision has been the encouragement of colleagues who have applied my theory to various specialized fields. Edward Berger, a biologist who later became dean of the faculty at Dartmouth, was indispensable in my successful application for a grant in 1990 from the Ethical, Legal, and Social Implications (ELSI) Section of the Human Genome Project to apply my moral theory to the ethical problems that were arising from that project. We assembled a diverse group of philosophers, biologists, physicians, and educators, and after four years of work, *Morality and the New Genetics* was published in 1996. Ed also found my theory helpful when we wrote the policy governing the conduct of research at Dartmouth.

My colleague Jim Moor encouraged me to apply my theory to ethical problems involved in computing. Since Jim is one of the most influential people working in the field of computer ethics, his enthusiasm for applying a version of my theory supported my view that my theory could be of use to people confronting ethical problems in all areas. Jim also read an early draft of this book and made valuable suggestions.

John Hennessey, former dean of the Tuck School of Business at Dartmouth College, encouraged me by collaborating with me on an article applying my theory to some problems in business ethics. Carolyn Fluehr-Lobban, an anthropologist who was a visiting Ethics Institute Fellow at Dartmouth for a year, worked on the application of my theory to anthropology. She later was instrumental in having me invited to consult with the anthropologists who were revising the anthropology code of ethics. My reception by this group gave me further encouragement that I had something of value to offer.

James Bernat, a neurologist and chair of the Ethics Advisory Committee at Dartmouth-Hitchcock Medical Center, not only collaborated with me on several articles in medical ethics but also used my theory in both editions of his own book, *Ethical Issues in Neurology*. More than twenty years on the ethics committee at Hitchcock Hospital was another factor that convinced me of the practical value of my account of morality.

I have also greatly benefited from help by two colleagues from the philosophy department of the University of New Hampshire, Timm Triplett and Paul McNamara. Timm taught a seminar on my book *Morality: Its Nature and Justification* in which I participated. He also wrote a review of that book in which he applied my theory, in a more detailed manner than I did, to the question of the moral acceptability of illegally copying software. His successful application was a great encouragement to me. I also benefited from his comments on drafts of this book. Paul used a draft of this book in his course and has provided me with some very helpful student reactions. Paul also sent me his own very detailed comments on that draft, which were extremely valuable. My continuing e-mail exchanges with him have been both challenging and encouraging. The analytical table of contents was Paul's idea.

Sheldon W. Samuels, former director of Health, Safety, and Environment for the industrial unions of the AFL-CIO and now vice president of The Ramazzini Institute for Occupational and Environmental Health Research, was one of the first persons to read an entire draft of this book, and his comments and suggestions have been quite valuable. I first met Sheldon at a conference of ELSI grantees and we each immediately recognized that we were thinking about ethical issues in ways that could be mutually beneficial. Sheldon's use of my theory in the work of the Ramazzini Institute gave me great confidence that my theory had real-world validity. Ted Bond, whom I have known since we were graduate students together at Cornell, not only provided a valuable contribution to the conference on my 1998 book but also provided me with extremely detailed and helpful comments on this book. Ted's critical reviews of my 1998 book and of an earlier version as well were also very important to me.

Other people have read over this manuscript and have offered valuable advice, but since I have not accepted all of their suggestions, they cannot be held responsible for the remaining errors and in-felicities. Vinit Haksar provided detailed comments on this book that were very helpful. Bob Ladenson provided me with such extremely cogent and detailed suggestions that I was forced to revise some material that I had not intended to revise at all. The comments of Donald Borchert and Michael Ridge were also valuable. Rabbi Edward Boraz supplied both encouragement and helpful comments. Robert Baum used a draft of this book in his large introductory ethics course at the University of Florida and made some valuable suggestions about its organization.

Charles M. Culver and the late K. Danner Clouser were the two persons with whom I have worked most closely in applying my moral theory to moral problems in medicine. For about thirty years, I collaborated with each of them in writing many articles, and the three of us also worked on *Bioethics: A Return to Fundamentals* (Oxford: Oxford University Press, 1997) for almost a decade before it was published. Those years of work resulted in many improvements, not only in the application of the theory but in the theory itself.

My sister, Ilene Wolosin helped me to improve the presentation and style of this book, making it more readily understandable to those who are not philosophers. My wife, Esther, not only enabled me to lead the kind of life that made it possible to spend so much time working on this book but even went over the final draft and made several very helpful suggestions. My children, Heather and Joshua, both of them excellent philosophers, have been urging me to write a short version of my theory for several years, but I had been reluctant to do so because I still was not confident that I was clear enough on all of the important points. However, Heather's account of rights clarified the relationship between rights and moral rules, and my acceptance of Joshua's criticisms of my account of rationality helped me to clarify the major remaining points of confusion.

My great pride in this book is not incompatible with the humility to accept the fact that without the help I have received from all of the people mentioned in these acknowledgments, and many others besides, this book might not even exist, let alone be as good as I now think it to be.

::

Acknowledgments for Paperback Edition

I am grateful to Andrew Alexandra and Seumas Miller, who pointed out the need to add the feature concerning duties in note 16 to part I, p. 164. See their article "Common Morality and 'Institutionalising' Ethics" in the *Australian Journal of Professional and Applied Ethics* 7, no. 2 (March 2006):1–19. I am grateful to Carson Strong for note 23 to part I, page 165. His essay "Gert's Moral Theory and Its Application to Bioethics Cases" (*Kennedy Institute of Ethics Journal* [March 2006]) pointed out the importance, when considering a paternalistic violation of a rule, of explicitly including in morally relevant feature 3 the rationality or irrationality of the decision of the person toward whom the rule is being violated and the rationality or irrationality of the (implied or explicit) ranking of the evils by that person. I am grateful to Brad Hooker for pointing out that impartiality is an even more complex concept than is presented in my definition. I try to acknowledge some of that complexity in note 21 to part II, page 169. My colleague Jim Moor has persuaded me to add to the list of goods (benefits) *resources* and *security*, for although they can be included in the concept of freedom, it seems clearer to list them separately. However, adding them to the list of goods does not require any addition to the list of evils (harms), for depriving people of resources or security is clearly included in what is meant by depriving them of freedom.

⠶ Contents

⠶ Introduction   3

Some Areas of Widespread Agreement   8

Distinguishing Features of Moral Judgments   10

Rationality and Human Nature   12

Areas of Moral Disagreement   13

Analogy between Morality and Grammar   15

Part I ⠶ The Moral System   19

Features of the Moral System   19

The Moral Rules   20

The Moral Ideals   22

General Characteristics of Moral Rules   26
   To whom do the rules apply?   26
   Whom do the moral rules protect?   28

Interpreting the Rules   29
   1. "Do not kill."   29
   2. "Do not cause pain."   31
   3. "Do not disable."   33
   4. "Do not deprive of freedom."   35
   5. "Do not deprive of pleasure."   38

Summary of the first five rules   40

  6. "Do not deceive."   40

  7. "Keep your promises."   42

  8. "Do not cheat."   44

  9. "Obey the law."   47

  10. "Do your duty."   50

Violations of Moral Rules Involve Liability to Punishment   53

Justifying Violations of the Moral Rules   55

The Two-Step Procedure for Justifying Violations
of the Moral Rules   58

  The first step: Using the morally relevant features to describe
  the act   58

    1. Which moral rule is being violated?   59

    2. Which evils or harms (including their kind, severity,
      probability, the length of time they will be suffered, and
      their distribution) are being (a) caused by the violation,
      (b) avoided (not caused) by the violation, or
      (c) prevented by the violation?   60

    3. What are the desires and beliefs of the person toward whom
      the rule is being violated?   62

      (a) What are the desires of the person toward whom the rule
        is being violated?   62

      (b) What are the beliefs of the person toward whom the rule
        is being violated?   63

    4. Is the relationship between the person violating the rule and
      the persons toward whom the rule is being violated such that
      the former sometimes has a duty to violate moral rules with
      regard to the latter independently of their consent?   65

    5. Which goods or benefits (including kind, degree, probability,
      duration, and distribution) are being promoted by the
      violation?   66

6. Is the rule being violated toward a person in order to prevent her from violating a moral rule when her violation would be (a) unjustified or (b) weakly justified?   67

7. Is the rule being violated toward a person because he has violated a moral rule (a) unjustifiably or (b) with a weak justification?   68

8. Are there any alternative actions or policies that would be morally preferable?   69

9. Is the violation being done intentionally or only knowingly?   70

10. Is the situation an emergency such that people are not likely to plan to be in that kind of situation?   72

Summary of morally relevant features   73

The second step: Estimating the consequences of everyone knowing that a kind of violation is allowed and that it is not allowed   74

Moral Virtues and Vices   76

Summary and Test   78

Part II ∷ The Moral Theory   81

The Justification of Morality   81

Characteristics of Moral Agents   87

Knowledge or Beliefs Required of All Moral Agents   88

Irrationality and Rationality   91

Rationality as Maximizing Satisfaction of Desires   95

Objectively Irrational Actions   97

Personally Irrational Actions   99

Reasons versus Motives   103

All Reasons Have Justifying Force   106

Reasons and Desires   111

Adequate Reasons   112

Rationality, Morality, and Self-Interest   114

Impartiality   116

Two Philosophical Attempts to Achieve Moral Impartiality   119

Justifying Moral Impartiality   122
   Why morality requires impartiality with respect
   to the moral rules   122
   The group with regard to which morality requires
   impartiality   126

Why Act Morally?   131

Morality as an Informal Public System   137

The Role of Governments in Settling Unresolvable
Moral Disagreements   139

Rights   142

The Consequences of Morality Not Always Providing
a Unique Correct Answer   145

A Complete Moral Theory   148

Conclusion   149

Flow Charts   151
   Rationality   151
   Morality   152

Glossary for Common Morality   153

Notes   161

Index   173

◫ Common Morality

❏ Introduction

This book presents a clear, coherent, and comprehensive description and explanation of common morality. It contains no new information about what kinds of actions morality prohibits, requires, discourages, encourages, or allows. Anyone who is intelligent enough to read this book already has all of this information; it would be absurd for anyone to offer as an excuse for acting immorally that they had not read this book, or any other book, including any religious text. However, if this book cannot present new moral prohibitions or requirements or rescind old ones, what can it do? Providing an explicit description of morality can help individuals decide what to do when faced with a difficult moral problem. Explaining how morality is related to rationality, impartiality, and human nature can provide a justification for morality. That is what I try to do with my description and explanation of morality. It is also what other philosophers, such as Kant and Mill, tried to do in their books.

It should be obvious that before explaining and justifying morality, it is necessary to have a clear, coherent, and comprehensive description of morality. Failure to have an explicit, detailed description makes it likely that what starts out as an explanation and justification of morality will end up being a revision of it as well. Because Kant and Mill did not begin with such a detailed description, they did end up providing revised versions of morality. As a result, people now talk about Kantian morality and Utilitarian morality, as if there were more than one morality. In this book, before I attempt to explain and justify common morality—that is, the moral system that thoughtful people implicitly use when making moral decisions and judgments—I present a detailed description of it. I do not revise common morality; I only describe, explain, and justify it.

If the only revisions of common morality were those put forward by philosophers like Kant and Mill, there would be little cause for concern. Few people read these philosophers, even fewer understand them, and almost no one uses what they say as a guide to their own behavior. However, revisions of morality have been put forward by many religions and these are a cause for concern. Many people do not distinguish between religious support for the prohibitions and requirements of common morality and the prohibitions and requirements peculiar to their own religion. Even the Ten Commandments, taken by many to be a list of the moral rules, contains rules that have nothing to do with morality—for instance, the commandment "Remember the Sabbath to keep it holy." Although every major religion endorses morality, there are many religions but only one morality. Because of the power of religious belief, the failure to distinguish between morality and religions has been the source of an incredible amount of immoral behavior.

As a practical matter, the most valuable consequence of a careful examination of morality and its relationship to our universal human nature is to show morality's independence from any particular religion. But the claim that morality is based solely on human nature does not mean that common morality provides a unique correct answer to every moral question. It is impossible to provide a description of morality that will both resolve every moral disagreement and also be endorsed by all rational persons.[1] Common morality is a framework or system that can help individuals decide what to do when faced with a moral problem, but within limits, it allows for divergent answers to most controversial questions. Recognizing that there are several morally acceptable answers to most controversial moral questions makes it less likely that people will believe that they themselves have the unique correct answer and that everyone else is mistaken. This may promote moral tolerance and far more fruitful discussions of moral questions.

Immoral behavior has been prohibited by every society for thousands of years. Every major religious tradition in every part of the world encourages morally good behavior. This agreement about the importance of morality is significant because there is also so much agreement about the content of morality. We all agree that killing people or causing them pain is immoral unless adequately justified, and we agree on many of the features of an adequate justification. We also agree that helping the needy is morally good. Any description of morality must explain this agreement. However, this agreement about morality must be reconciled with the fact that not only do different societies seem to have different moral codes, but even within a single society, rational people often disagree about what morally ought to be done.

The most persuasive argument in favor of ethical relativism, the view that equally informed rational persons need not agree on the answer to *any* moral question, is the falsity of the view that all equally informed rational persons must agree on the answer to *every* moral question. Similarly, the most persuasive argument in favor of the view that all equally informed rational people must agree on the answer to every moral question is the falsity of the view that such people need not agree on the answer to any moral question. Although both of these views are correct in their appraisal of the other, this does not count in their favor. The commonsense and correct view is that although all rational people will agree on the answers to most moral questions, they need not agree on the answers to all of them. This is shown by the tolerance that those who are not extremists have with regard to people who hold different views than they do on controversial topics such as abortion and the treatment of animals. Common morality, the moral system that rational persons use, usually implicitly, when making their moral decisions and judgments, allows for impartial rational persons to sometimes disagree on how people morally ought to behave. Common morality not only explains the overwhelming agreement concerning most moral decisions and judgments but also explains why there is some unresolvable moral disagreement.

Examination of the content of common morality makes it clear that it is a system that it would be rational for all persons to want everyone to be taught and trained to follow because of the protection that it provides for themselves and for those for whom they are concerned. This is true of all persons, whether they are egoists, are concerned only with family and friends, or are equally concerned for everyone. It is rational for all persons to want everyone to obey rules such as "Do not kill," "Do not deceive," and "Keep your promises" with regard to themselves and those for whom they are concerned. Contrary to the views put forward by some philosophers, morality need not be a system that people adopt as a guide for their own behavior; it is a system that rational persons put forward as a public guide for the behavior of everyone who can understand it and guide their behavior by it, that is, all moral agents.

Although it is rational (rationally allowed) for people to endorse the practice and teaching of morality, it is also rational for them not to adopt it as a guide for their own conduct. Hypocrisy is rational. Not only is it rational for people not to genuinely adopt the moral guide to conduct that they publicly endorse, it is sometimes even rational for them not to openly endorse the practice and teaching of morality. Members of a dominant group may be acting rationally if they do not advocate treating members of a subordinate group morally. However, it also is rational for them to advocate that everyone act morally toward all moral agents. Furthermore, although it is usually not irrational to act immorally, it is never irrational to act as morality encourages or requires.

Of course, many rational persons adopt morality as a guide for their own behavior, but this does not explain why all rational persons care about others accepting morality as their guide. They care because immoral actions by others often have bad consequences for them and those they care about. Morality, in the basic sense with which I am concerned, guides behavior only insofar as that behavior, directly or indirectly, affects other people. The point of morality is to lessen the suffering of those harms that all rational persons want to avoid: death, pain, disability, loss of freedom, and loss of pleasure. Moral rules are the aspect of morality that seeks to lessen these harms by prohibiting those actions that cause them or cause an increased risk of them. Moral ideals are the aspect of morality that directly encourages lessening these harms. The moral system also includes a two-step procedure that includes a guide for determining what counts as the same kind of violation and that involves estimating the harm that would result from everyone knowing that this kind of violation of a moral rule is allowed and that it is not allowed. This procedure is used when moral rules conflict or when a moral ideal conflicts with a moral rule.

As my description of common morality will make clear, it is far more complex and subtle than the systems of conduct that most philosophers, such as Kant and Mill, generate from their moral theories, and that are often taken as an improvement upon common morality. None of the standard moral theories provide anything close to an adequate description of common morality. Even the best of these theories, including those of Hobbes, Kant, and Mill, provide only a schematic outline that greatly oversimplifies the moral system that is commonly used. Although morality is complex, this complexity, like the complexity of the grammar of a language, does not conflict with its being understood by all moral agents. It is an essential feature of common morality that all moral agents understand what kind of behavior it prohibits, requires, discourages, encourages, and allows.[2] Indeed, a person is not a moral agent if he does not understand what kind of behavior morality prohibits, requires, discourages, encourages, and allows. Further, a person is not subject to moral judgment in a particular case if she could not have known that morality prohibited her action. This distinguishes morality from law and religion. A person is subject to legal judgment even if she could not have known that the law prohibited her action. Similarly, a person is subject to religious judgment even if she could not have known that her religion prohibited her action.

Common morality's complexity and subtlety cannot be shown merely by examining its general features; it is also necessary to make explicit many of its specific details. Its nature is explained by relating it to the universal features of human nature such as fallibility, vulnerability, and rationality, and these features are also used to justify it. Describing the relevant aspects of human nature and of morality, and clarifying their intimate relation to each other, should make it obvious why, under conditions to be specified later, all rational persons favor adopting common morality as a public system that applies to everyone. The moral theory presented in this book is not used to generate an improved system of conduct; rather, it is an attempt to describe, explain, and justify our common morality.

⠶

Some Areas of Widespread Agreement

The existence of a common morality is supported by the widespread agreement on most moral matters by all moral agents.[3] Insofar as they do not use any beliefs that are not shared by all moral agents, they all agree that killing, causing pain or disability, or depriving of freedom or pleasure any other moral agent is immoral unless there is an adequate justification for doing such an action.[4] Similarly, they all agree that deceiving, breaking promises, cheating, breaking the law, and neglecting duties also need justification in order not to be immoral. There are no real doubts about these matters. The claim that there are moral rules prohibiting such actions as killing and deceiving means only that these kinds of actions are immoral unless they can be justified. Given this understanding, all moral agents agree that there are moral rules prohibiting such actions as killing and deceiving.

All moral agents also agree that such actions as saving lives, relieving or preventing pain, curing or preventing disabilities, and preventing the loss of freedom or pleasure are morally good actions unless doing them involves violating a moral rule. Saying that there are moral ideals encouraging such actions as saving lives and preventing pain means only that these kinds of actions are usually morally encouraged. When acting on a moral ideal involves violating a moral rule, rational persons sometimes disagree about what morally should be done. Although it is clear that you should tell a lie in order to save an innocent person's life, it is often not clear whether you should tell a lie simply in order to prevent someone from feeling bad. One of the main points of this book is to provide a procedure for properly describing the kind of action under consideration so that people can make better moral decisions and judgments.

In addition to general agreement about the kinds of actions that are immoral unless justified (violations of moral rules) and the kinds of actions that are often morally good (acting on moral ideals), there is also agreement about some essential features of an adequate justification. There is universal agreement that what counts as an adequate justification for one person to break a moral rule also counts as a justification for all other persons when the violation has all of the same morally relevant features. What leads some people to think that they doubt this is their failure to realize that one of the morally relevant features of an action involves the relationship between the violator of the moral rule and the person(s) with respect to whom she is violating the rule.

A mother is morally allowed to break the rule prohibiting depriving of freedom with regard to her own children only in circumstances in which all mothers are justified in breaking that rule with regard to their own children in those same circumstances. A mother may be allowed to break the rule prohibiting depriving of freedom with regard to her own children when she would not be allowed to break the rule with regard to children with whom she does not have that relationship. This does not militate against the view that when the violation has all of the same morally relevant features, what counts as an adequate justification for one person also counts as an adequate justification for all other persons. Doubts about the importance of impartiality with regard to obeying moral rules are based on mistaken descriptions of the concept of impartiality, including the impartiality required by morality. An analysis of impartiality will be provided in part II.

⠶
Distinguishing Features of Moral Judgments

The most important distinguishing feature of moral judgments has been generally ignored, even though there is general agreement about it. It is that moral judgments are appropriately made only about the actions of people insofar as they are capable of understanding what kinds of actions morality prohibits, requires, discourages, encourages, and allows. No one makes moral judgments about the actions of nonhuman animals, even such intelligent animals as chimpanzees and dolphins. Although we praise animals for actions that would count as morally good if done by moral agents, and we punish animals for actions that would count as immoral if done by moral agents, moral judgments are not made about the actions of non-human animals. Nor are moral judgments made about the actions of infants and young children, nor about people who are severely retarded, even though we may praise and punish these people for their actions. Whether moral judgments should be made about the actions of older children depends on whether they are capable of understanding that morality prohibits or requires those kinds of actions.

Contrary to what is suggested by the writings of many philosophers, "morally bad," "morally good," "morally ought," "morally right," and "morally wrong" are not redundant phrases. They do not mean the same as "bad," "good," "ought," "right," and "wrong." As an examination of the ordinary uses of the latter terms shows, most of them have nothing to do with morality—for example, "That is a good movie; you ought to go see it." The failure to appreciate this fact is responsible for the apparent plausibility of views that have no plausibility at all. Moral judgments are not made about actions on the basis of the good or bad consequences about which the agent is legitimately and totally ignorant. Even less controversial is the view that moral judgments are not made about actions on the basis of the good or bad consequences about which, at the time of acting, no one could have known. A completely unexpected fluke that results in an action that saves many people's lives does not make the action *morally* good. Similarly, a completely unexpected fluke that results in an action that causes many people to die does not make the action *morally* bad. The former action is lucky, the latter a tragedy, but neither of them is the proper subject of a moral judgment on the basis of consequences that were completely unknowable at the time of acting.

Common morality incorporates all of these areas of widespread agreement. A detailed description of common morality provides a framework that all parties to a moral dispute can accept, even though they may disagree with each other on what morally ought to be done in a particular case. Common morality is not a system that can be mechanically applied to resolve all controversial moral issues. Not all controversial moral issues can be resolved.

⠛

Rationality and Human Nature

These areas of widespread agreement are the result of some universal facts about human nature. All human beings are vulnerable; not only can they suffer all the harms mentioned, but they can be caused to suffer these harms by the actions of others. People can be killed, caused to suffer pain, be disabled, and be deprived of freedom and pleasure by the actions of other people. No rational person wants to suffer any of these harms unless he has an adequate reason for suffering it. In fact, all rational persons seek to avoid death, pain, disability, loss of freedom, and loss of pleasure unless they have an adequate reason not to avoid them. Thus, it is not surprising that it is rational for them to favor the adoption of rules that prohibit causing such harms to themselves and those for whom they are concerned.

However, rational persons may be prepared to suffer any of these harms if they have an adequate reason to do so. They sometimes undergo serious painful procedures in order to postpone death; however, they also sometimes choose to die more quickly in order to avoid continuing pain and suffering. Within limits, rational persons often differ in their rankings of the different harms. Although they agree on the basic kinds of things that are harms or evils, in particular circumstances they often disagree about which evil, for example, death or pain, counts as worse. Further, some rational persons may choose to suffer serious harm or risk of harm in order to prevent or relieve other people from suffering even more serious harm. Often, as shown most dramatically in the case of firemen, these are people that they do not even know. Even those rational persons who are not motivated to help others, or at least any persons outside their group of friends, do not regard those who risk harm to help others avoid serious harm as acting irrationally.

In addition to being vulnerable, people are also fallible. They not only have limited knowledge but often make mistakes. All moral agents agree about some general features of our world, for example, that it exists and that there are other people like them in it. They know that, like them, other people are vulnerable, want to avoid harm, and are fallible. But there are many disagreements about other matters, for example, the origin of the world. People also often disagree not only about what will happen but also about what has happened and even about what is happening now. But although memories and even perception are sometimes mistaken, they are reliable enough to allow people to survive and reproduce. People often know what they are doing and what the short-term effects of their actions will be. However, everyone is aware that even people who are confident that they are correct are sometimes mistaken.

⠶ Areas of Moral Disagreement

In everyday life, most moral disagreement is due to disagreement about the facts, including facts about the probability of the consequences of the proposed action and of alternative courses of action. Over two decades on a hospital ethics committee has shown me that the popular view that people agree about the facts but disagree about values is almost completely mistaken. Once agreement on the facts is obtained, including agreement about the consequences of an action and its alternatives, most moral disagreement ceases. However, some controversial topics like physician-assisted suicide are such that even when there is complete agreement on the facts, there is still moral disagreement. These topics are so controversial and generate so much discussion that many are led to the false view that moral questions are always controversial. However, moral questions such as whether it is morally acceptable to hurt someone simply because you dislike him are not controversial at all, but because they generate no discussion they tend to be forgotten.

All of the causes of unresolvable moral disagreement that are not based on unresolvable disagreement about the facts can be classified into four categories. These four kinds of unresolvable differences will be discussed in more detail in the second part of this book concerning the justification of morality.

1. Differences concerning who besides moral agents are impartially protected, or protected at all, by morality. These differences, particularly whether a fetus is impartially protected, partially protected, or not protected at all, are responsible for some of the most serious disagreements. Although all the arguments on both sides of the dispute about the moral acceptability of abortion have been presented without convincing those on the other side, both sides seem reluctant to admit that this dispute is unresolvable. However, except for extremists, who use beliefs that would not be acceptable to all rational persons, and who are condemned by both sides, all agree that it is not morally justifiable to violate moral rules toward those who take the opposite view in order to prevent them from acting on their views. Although less widespread, there are similar differences about the degree to which morality provides protection to animals, especially mammals such as chimpanzees and dolphins.

2. Differences in the rankings of the various harms and benefits, such as whether reducing the risk of being killed or injured

by a specified amount outweighs a specified loss of freedom, for example, whether it is morally justified to have a law requiring everyone to wear seat belts. Many political disagreements involve different rankings of loss of freedom versus prevention of other harms. These disagreements by themselves are often significant, but they may also involve disagreements about the facts of the particular case. They may also involve the kind of difference that is the third category of unresolvable differences.

3. Differences in the estimates of the harmful and beneficial consequences of everyone knowing that a given kind of violation is allowed and that it is not allowed. People sometimes differ in their estimates of the consequences of everyone knowing that deception is allowed when the deceiver has good reasons to believe that no one will be harmed by that deception. An example is lying to a person to prevent hurting her feelings. These differences often involve views about human nature, and insofar as they cannot be empirically settled, they should be regarded as ideological disagreements.

4. Differences about whether the action is of a kind that would be immoral if not justified. I talk about these differences as differences in the interpretations of moral rules. If a ventilator-dependent patient has validly refused to continue being on a respirator, does taking him off of the respirator count as killing him? The basis for this difference in interpretation is one or more of the three previous kinds of differences. One of the primary tasks of applied and professional ethics is to interpret the rules in a particular setting, such as what kinds of actions in this setting count as deceiving or killing.

⠶
Analogy between Morality and Grammar

Common morality is complex, but it is less complex than the grammar of a language. Just as all and only speakers of a language who can use its grammar in speaking intelligibly and in understanding the speech of others are considered to be competent, so all and only those persons who can apply the moral system in making moral decisions and judgments are considered moral agents. However, only those who have tried to systematize and explain the utterances of competent speakers, such as grammarians, can provide an explicit description of the grammatical system. Similarly, only those who attempt to systematize and explain the thoughtful moral decisions and judgments of moral agents, such as philosophers, can provide an explicit description of the moral system that accounts for those decisions and judgments.

Grammarians make explicit the rules of grammar that competent speakers of the language make use of implicitly in speaking and interpreting the speech of others. The test of whether these explicit grammatical rules are the implicit rules used by competent speakers is determined by whether they yield the sentences that these competent speakers accept as grammatical and rule out the sentences that these competent speakers reject as ungrammatical. Although there are many languages, some linguists claim that there is a universal grammar that provides the framework for all languages.

Similarly, moral philosophers attempt to make explicit the moral rules, ideals, and procedures for justifying violations that moral agents make use of implicitly in making their own moral decisions and judging the moral decisions of others. Common morality provides the universal framework for all the moral codes of particular societies. The test of whether the system made explicit by a philosopher is this framework is whether it yields the decisions and judgments that all moral agents accept as morally acceptable and rules out those decisions and judgments that all moral agents reject as unacceptable. However, since moral decisions and judgments involve our interests and emotions to a much greater extent than deciding whether a sentence is grammatical, moral agents sometimes make moral decisions and judgments that conflict with the implicit system that they normally use in making their moral decisions and judgments. Indeed, sometimes they are so emotionally invested in a particular decision or judgment, for example, because of their religious beliefs, that they may even explicitly repudiate the implicit system that guides their other moral decisions and judgments. I do not take these judgments to count at all against my description of common morality.

Grammarians do not have the final word on what counts as a grammatical sentence. Unlike historians or scientists, who can prove that everyone is mistaken in what they take to be a historical or scientific fact, grammarians cannot show everyone to be mistaken in their understanding of grammar. Competent speakers of a language have the final word on what counts as a grammatical sentence. Philosophers are closer to grammarians than to historians and scientists. However, morality must be a consistent system, all of whose parts must be rationally acceptable. Therefore, a philosopher can show that a moral decision or judgment that is made by a large number of moral agents is mistaken if he can show that the decision (or acting according to the judgment) is irrational. Also, given agreement on the facts, a moral philosopher can show that a moral decision or judgment is mistaken if he can show that the moral decision or judgment is incompatible with the moral decisions or judgments that would be made by any impartial rational person.[5]

Part I ∷ The Moral System

∷
Features of the Moral System

Although moral rules and moral ideals are the most recognizable elements of common morality, the moral system is not merely a collection of moral rules and ideals; it is the system in which these rules and ideals are embedded. This system also includes a two-step procedure that people use, usually implicitly, to decide whether to allow a particular violation of a moral rule. The first step is describing a violation in terms of a set of morally relevant features, thereby determining the correct description of the violation. The second step is estimating the harmful and beneficial consequences of everyone knowing that the violation described by means of the first step is allowed.[1]

The moral rules, moral ideals, and a two-step procedure, including the morally relevant features, for deciding whether a violation of a moral rule is justified are the central features of the common moral system. If my description of common morality is correct, all those who conscientiously apply the following explicit description of the moral system to moral problems will discover that they agree with the moral decisions and judgments that result. This does not mean that everyone who correctly applies this moral system will make the same moral decisions and judgments. Although there will be agreement on the moral acceptability of a vast majority of actions, common morality allows for some unresolvable moral disagreements.

Common morality is a framework that, within limits, allows different persons to fill in their own view about (1) the scope of morality, (2) the rankings of the relevant harms and benefits, (3) the harmful and beneficial consequences of everyone knowing that a given kind of violation is allowed and that it is not allowed, and (4) the interpretation of the rules. When a rational person incorporates her views on these matters into the common moral framework, the moral system will yield those moral decisions and judgments that the person accepts, at least after reflection.[2] If it does not, then I will have been shown wrong and my description of morality will have to be revised again.

::

The Moral Rules

The ten general moral rules listed below account for all of the kinds of actions that are morally prohibited and required. They make explicit that part of the moral system that informs moral agents if some excuse or justification is needed for their behavior. They are formulated to provide a clear and usable description of that part of the moral system.

1. Do not kill.	6. Do not deceive.
2. Do not cause pain.	7. Keep your promises.
3. Do not disable.	8. Do not cheat.
4. Do not deprive of freedom.	9. Obey the law.
5. Do not deprive of pleasure.	10. Do your duty.

All violations of any of these rules without adequate justification are immoral actions. Given the appropriate interpretations, these rules also prohibit all immoral actions. All of these rules should be interpreted not only as prohibiting any intentional violation of a rule but also as prohibiting any attempt to violate a rule, even if that attempt is unsuccessful. Not only are causing pain and deceiving violations, but so is attempting to cause pain and deceive. Intentionally acting so as to significantly increase the risk that someone will suffer any harm also counts as a violation of these rules. All of these violations are immoral unless the agent has an adequate justification for the violation. Knowingly, but not intentionally, sometimes even unknowingly, acting in a way that results in someone suffering a harm or in a significantly increased risk of someone suffering a harm sometimes counts as a violation of a rule, but sometimes not. Whether it does depends on the circumstances of the case and the interpretation of the rule.

Other formulations of moral rules might also prohibit all immoral actions, but the present formulation is both natural and has less serious problems than other commonly proposed formulations. The first five rules could be collapsed into one rule, "Do not cause harm," but this would give the false impression that harms are a homogenous category that can be ranked on a single scale. Of course, the rule "Do not cause pain" could also be criticized on the same grounds, but the explicit recognition that there are several different kinds of harms makes it unlikely as well as pointless to claim that everyone ranks all pains in the same way. Although it is obvious that different kinds of pains are ranked differently by different people, there are too many kinds of pain to have a separate rule that prohibits causing each of them. Having one rule that prohibits causing all pains, together with having distinct rules that prohibit causing each of the four other general kinds of harms, does not suggest that everyone agrees on the ranking of harms, but it allows five rules to prohibit causing all of the basic harms.

Collapsing all of the second five rules into some rule like "Do not violate trust" also would not be useful. Although this rule could be given a sense such that it prohibits every action prohibited by the second five rules, no one who was not taught this special sense would understand it. It would have to be explained by pointing out that it prohibits deceiving, breaking promises, cheating, breaking the law, and neglecting one's duty. Although each of the second five rules must also be explained, these explanations are generally quite straightforward and easily understood. As formulated, the ten rules are part of an explicit system that all moral agents can be expected to know and follow.[3]

Having ten moral rules, as this formulation does, takes advantage of a well-known tradition. That putting forward exactly ten rules leads some philosophers to try that much harder to find mistakes is an unintended bonus. The present formulation also results in the rules being neatly divided into two distinct categories, the first five prohibiting directly causing all of the basic harms and the second five prohibiting those kinds of actions that indirectly cause these same harms. Although widespread violation of the second five rules always results in an increase in the amount of harm suffered, a particular violation of the second five rules does not always result in anyone suffering some harm. Because no one may be harmed by a particular unjustifiable violation of any one of the second five rules, it is not surprising that it is primarily with regard to these rules that people ask, "Why should I be moral?"

The Moral Ideals

Since acting on any moral ideal is intentionally acting so as to avoid, prevent, or relieve the suffering of harm by someone protected by the moral system, there is no need to provide a detailed description of each particular moral ideal. Unlike the moral rules, people are only encouraged, not required, to follow moral ideals.

That means that failing to follow a moral ideal, unlike violating a moral rule, does not involve liability to punishment. Also, unlike violations of moral rules, which always need to be justified, there is usually no need to be concerned with justifying a failure to follow a moral ideal. As these considerations suggest, it is considered more important for people to obey the moral rules than to follow the moral ideals. In the final chapter of *Utilitarianism* (paragraph 32), Mill makes this point forcefully: "The moral rules which forbid mankind to hurt one another (in which we must never forget to include a wrongful interference with each other's freedom) are more vital to human well-being than any maxims, however important, which only point out the best mode of managing some department of human affairs. . . . a person may possibly not need the benefits of others, but he always needs that they not do him hurt."[4]

The moral ideals encourage people to prevent or relieve the harms that the moral rules prohibit them from causing. When a person has no duty to do so, it is following a moral ideal to prevent death, to prevent or relieve pain, to prevent or relieve disabilities, and to prevent the loss of freedom or the loss of pleasure. Preventing avoidable death, pain, and disability are among the major goals of medicine, which is why entering into the practice of medicine is usually regarded as following moral ideals. Insofar as lawyers seek to prevent the loss of freedom, they are also following moral ideals. Besides these direct attempts to prevent or relieve the suffering of harms, there are also indirect attempts. For example, police who seek to prevent people from unjustifiably violating the moral rules are acting on moral ideals—as are those who teach people to follow the moral rules and to act on the moral ideals. To intentionally act to lessen the amount of harm suffered by others, either directly or indirectly, is to follow a moral ideal, but such an action is not morally acceptable if it involves an unjustified violation of a moral rule.

When acting on a moral ideal involves violating a moral rule, it is often not clear whether the moral ideal should be followed or the moral rule obeyed. It may be thought that because people are required to obey the moral rules and are only encouraged to follow the moral ideals, following a moral ideal never justifies violating a moral rule. Stated abstractly, it may sound paradoxical to say that doing what is morally encouraged can justify not doing what is morally required, but examples show its truth. Unless he has an adequate justification, a person who promises to pick someone up for dinner is morally required to do so. No person, except possibly a fireman, is required to risk his life to save children from a burning building. Nonetheless, assuming that such a risk is reasonable, many would morally encourage a person to try to save the children. However, if he were no more qualified than many others who were also present, he would certainly not be morally required to do so. Yet no one doubts that his trying to save the children provides an adequate justification for his breaking his promise to pick up the person for dinner.

Because following a moral ideal can provide a justification for violating a moral rule, it is important to distinguish moral ideals from other ideals that do not provide such a justification. In particular, it is important to distinguish moral ideals, which aim at lessening the amount of harm suffered, from utilitarian ideals, which aim at increasing the amount of goods. Usually there is no doubt about whether a person is following a moral ideal or a utilitarian ideal (physicians act on moral ideals; pastry chefs act on utilitarian ideals), but sometimes it is not clear which is involved. Providing pleasure for deprived persons counts as following a moral ideal, but providing more pleasure for those who already have a good life is following a utilitarian ideal.

The distinction between moral and utilitarian ideals loses its significance when it is not clear which one is involved. When an action is difficult to classify, it may not make any difference which way it is classified. Consider a case where a person has won a lottery but needs to claim her prize within a limited time or lose it.[5] Is it following a utilitarian ideal, promoting benefits, or a moral ideal, preventing the loss of benefits, to try to notify her so that she can claim the prize within the allotted time? To attempt to decide in this way whether it is justified to break a promise to pick up a friend for dinner in order to find and notify the lottery winner is to demand more precision than the subject matter allows. Although cases might be found in which following a utilitarian ideal is taken as justifying the violation of a moral rule, in almost all of these cases, it is also plausible to view the action as following a moral ideal. Or, because most of these cases involve breaking promises, it is likely that people justifiably believe that the person to whom the promise was made would have excused them from keeping the promise if she had known about the situation.

Like the actions prohibited or required by the basic general moral rules, the actions encouraged by the basic general moral ideals are simple kinds of actions, such as preventing or relieving pain, which are understood by all moral agents. But whereas the moral rules provide limits to what a person is allowed to do, no matter what his goals are, the moral ideals set out goals or ends that persons are encouraged to adopt. Whereas people are expected to abide by the limits set by the moral rules all of the time unless they have an adequate justification for violating them, no one is expected to try to achieve the goals or ends encouraged by the moral ideals all of the time. As will be explained by the analysis of impartiality in part II, whereas people are required to obey the moral rules impartially, they are not even encouraged to follow the moral ideals impartially. It is not morally better to distribute your money impartially among every worthy charity rather than to give that same amount to one or two worthy charities to which you have some special relationship.

NORTHEAST WISCONSIN TECHNICAL COLLEG
LIBRARY - 2740 W MASON ST
GREEN BAY, WI 54307

As both Kant and Mill point out, it is far more important for there to be general obedience to the moral rules (perfect duties) than for there to be general following of the moral ideals (imperfect duties). Whereas widespread failure to follow moral ideals prevents a society from flourishing, widespread violations of the moral rules make it impossible to maintain a viable society. Nonetheless, following the moral ideals expresses the point of morality, namely, the prevention of harm being suffered, more directly than obeying the moral rules. A person who never follows any moral ideals cannot be a morally good person, even if he never violates a moral rule. A hermit might never violate a moral rule, but this need not say anything about his moral character. Although a society could not continue to exist if there were not general obedience to the moral rules, it could not flourish unless a significant number of its citizens followed the moral ideals. Recognition of the importance of moral ideals makes clear that it is a serious mistake to regard morality as consisting solely of rules that prohibit and require. Nonetheless, the rules are central to morality, and so a more detailed analysis of them is in order.

::
General Characteristics of Moral Rules

To whom do the rules apply?

It is a general feature of all of the moral rules that they apply to all and only those persons who know them and can guide their conduct accordingly. Such people are moral agents. It is not appropriate to make moral judgments about people who are not moral agents. Only human beings are known to be moral agents, but not all human beings are moral agents. Infants and very young children are not moral agents, because they do not understand the rules. Older children who can understand some of these rules are partial moral agents. People who are so severely retarded that they cannot understand any of the rules are not moral agents, and people who have such serious mental disorders that they cannot guide their conduct by the rules are also not subject to moral judgments. As noted earlier, even people who are moral agents are not subject to moral judgments for their actions when those actions are not violations of the second five moral rules and they are completely excusably ignorant of the harmful consequences of their actions. A driver of a car is not subject to an adverse moral judgment if, while driving with due diligence, his car runs over a piece of metal and sends it flying into the air and it hits a person and seriously injures him. Saying that a person is completely excused is not making a moral judgment about his action; it is saying that making a moral judgment is inappropriate.

To know the moral rules is to know what kinds of actions they prohibit and require. No moral agent who is a member of a society is ignorant of the basic general moral rules. All moral agents know that killing another moral agent, causing him pain or disability, or depriving him of freedom or pleasure is immoral unless there is an adequate justification for doing so. Similarly, all moral agents know that deceiving, breaking a promise, cheating, disobeying the law, and neglecting one's duty are immoral if not adequately justified. There is very little disagreement about what counts as a moral rule. Mill explicitly states that even most philosophers accept the same moral rules (*Utilitarianism*, chapter 1, paragraph 3). However, since there often are adequate justifications for breaking any of these moral rules, disagreements about when a person morally should violate a moral rule are more common.

Whom do the moral rules protect?

Although some religions such as Jainism prohibit causing harm to bacteria, plants, or insects, common morality does not. It is universally agreed that violating the moral rules with regard to any moral agent must be justified.[6] Infants and very young children are not moral agents but are almost universally regarded as having the full protection of the moral rules.[7] I use the term "person" to refer to those whom all moral agents or almost all moral agents regard as being impartially protected by the moral rules, especially the first five. Whether fetuses are protected by these moral rules and, if so, at what stage, whether from conception or from viability or from some other stage, is a matter of great controversy. Controversy also arises when considering killing some animals, particularly mammals, and especially those mammals that seem to have a rich mental life, such as chimpanzees and dolphins.[8] When these mammals are regarded as having a kind of mental life that approximates the kind of mental life that humans have, they are more likely to be regarded as being fully protected by the first five moral rules. However, there is much disagreement about this matter.

Kant seems to hold that only moral agents are fully protected, whereas Bentham, Mill's mentor, explicitly claims that any being capable of suffering pain is fully protected. Common morality does not favor either side of this disagreement. Both views are within the common moral framework, even if only barely. Although there is almost complete agreement that infants and children who are too young to be moral agents are fully protected, moral agents disagree on any extension beyond that. Moral agents agree that, if forced to choose between causing harm to a person and causing a similar harm to any nonhuman animal, it is immoral to cause harm to a person. However, even if nonpersons are not impartially protected, it is still widely held that morality does protect sentient beings to some extent, especially those mammals that seem to have a rich mental life.

With regard to the second five moral rules, it is much less plausible that they protect more than moral agents. Although it is possible to deceive animals, unless that deception results in their suffering some harm, including a loss of trust, it is implausible to claim that it is morally wrong to do so. It is doubtful that one can even break promises to animals or cheat them, and even if one can, it seems that there is nothing immoral about doing so unless the animal will suffer some harm because of that. With regard to the second five moral rules, there seems to be a satisfying symmetry in holding that, unless some harm is caused, these moral rules protect only those who have the characteristics that require them to follow the rules. However, with regard to the first five rules prohibiting causing harm, especially the rule prohibiting causing pain, common morality recognizes that the protection of the moral rules may be extended far beyond moral agents and even persons. Some hold that the rule prohibiting causing pain protects all sentient beings almost as much as it protects moral agents, while others hold that only completely pointless causing of pain to such beings is morally prohibited. The extent of morality's protection is a matter of significant unresolvable disagreement.

⠶
Interpreting the Rules

1. "Do not kill."

The rule prohibiting killing is regarded by most as the clearest and most straightforward moral rule. "Do not kill" is included on all standard lists of moral rules. Except when suffering from untreatable severe pain or other suffering, death seems to most people to be the most serious of all harms. It may seem obvious that the loss of life is the most serious loss a person can suffer, but unless one has some relevant religious belief, reflection makes it clear that simply being alive is not something that has any value in itself. It is the permanent loss of consciousness that is important. No one values being alive when in a persistent vegetative state, a state in which a person is able to breathe on her own but in which she has completely and permanently lost all consciousness, that is, has no mental life at all. Being alive is a necessary condition for being conscious, but it is being conscious, not life without consciousness, that people value. Thus, the rule against killing should be interpreted as prohibiting causing the permanent loss of consciousness, even without causing death. Causing temporary loss of consciousness is prohibited by the rule "Do not disable."

Although the rule "Do not disable" prohibits causing the permanent loss of consciousness, "Do not kill" remains the standard formulation because the permanent loss of consciousness is almost always caused only by death. The interpretation of the rule against killing, however, has caused some serious problems. Turning off the respirator of a ventilator-dependent patient with the result that the patient dies may seem to be a clear case of killing. However, if a competent, adequately informed terminally ill patient freely refuses further ventilator support, then her refusal is valid, and turning off the respirator by an authorized person does not count as killing. Rather, it counts as allowing the patient to die. This is shown by the fact that all states prohibit euthanasia (or mercy killing), and almost all prohibit even physician-assisted suicide, but not only do all states explicitly allow turning off the respirator when a competent patient validly refuses to be on it any longer, but they all require doing so. Executing a prisoner is clearly a violation of the rule against killing, and so needs to be justified.

2. "Do not cause pain."

Unless they have some reason, every rational person wants any painful sensation or feeling to stop; painful sensations and feelings are just those sensations and feelings that rational persons want to stop feeling. Physical pain is a painful sensation that, unless they have some reason, every rational person wants to end immediately if not sooner. Different kinds of unpleasant feelings have characteristic kinds of behavior and facial expressions as part of their criterian.[9] Physical pain involves wincing, while anger and other kinds of displeasure involve frowning. The characteristic expressions of disgust, fear, and sadness are also well known.[10] There is usually no doubt when someone is suffering any of these unpleasant feelings. Of course, there are many instances in which a person wants to have these unpleasant feelings, for example, when riding on a roller coaster or when watching a horror film or a film that makes you want to cry. In these cases, there is a reason for wanting to have the unpleasant feelings, even though it is often difficult to formulate exactly what that reason is. In any event, people do not want others to cause them to have painful sensations and feelings unless they have given their consent.

In order to account for all of our moral judgments, the rule that prohibits causing pain must be understood to prohibit causing mental pain as well as physical pain and also to prohibit causing such unpleasant feelings as anger (and lesser kinds of displeasure), fear (anxiety), disgust, and sadness.[11] Using "pain" to refer to all unpleasant feelings is fairly standard and should cause no misunderstandings. However, the fact that it is so common for people to act in ways that result in other people having some unpleasant feelings raises a general problem that affects the interpretations of all of the moral rules. Every intentional causing of any harm, including any of these unpleasant feelings, counts as a violation of a rule and needs to be justified. However, when a person does not intend to cause any harm, it is sometimes not clear under what circumstances her action counts as violating the rule even though someone suffers harm as a result of it. Sometimes the person may not only not have intended for anyone to have any unpleasant feelings but also not even have known that any unpleasant feelings would result from her action. Sometimes she could not even have been expected to know.

Suppose that a teacher knows that giving a student a well-deserved flunking grade will result in his feeling bad, but it is not her intention to cause him to feel bad. Is that a violation of this rule? What about a doctor who in a very gentle and compassionate way gives her patient bad news about his disease? Or consider a student in a school with an honor system who reports a student who has cheated on an exam. These are cases when persons know that bad feelings or other harms will result, but causing them is not their intention. There are other cases when a person does not even know that bad feelings will result, such as reporting some well-documented piece of news that unexpectedly makes some people feel bad. Seemingly closely related is passing along a piece of gossip that unexpectedly makes some people feel bad. Another common example is telling a joke that unexpectedly offends one of the listeners. Some of these cases may count as violating the moral rule that prohibits causing pain and it is important to decide which they are and why. This is one of those issues about which a moral theory can be of some help, and it will be discussed when the justification of morality is presented.[12]

When a person is completely excusably ignorant that her action would result in anyone having bad feelings, and she is not violating any of the second five moral rules, not only should she not be blamed for her action, but no moral judgment at all should be made about her action. Complete excuses rule out all moral judgments on the action. Partial excuses are compatible with moral judgments being made about the action, and often affect the moral judgment made about the agent. Although moral judgments are inappropriate, a completely excusable violation of a moral rule by a moral agent is still a violation of a moral rule, and compensation may be legally required for the victim of the violation. For example, even though a driver of a car may not be morally responsible for causing an injury, so that no moral judgment is legitimate, he may still be legally required to compensate the injured party. However, similar harms caused by infants and animals are not even violations of the rule. Only moral agents can violate moral rules; neither infants nor animals can do so. This is why only moral agents can violate a person's rights, for to violate a person's rights is to violate a moral rule with regard to him without his consent.[13]

3. "Do not disable."

This rule could be formulated as "Do not deprive of ability," which would make it more closely resemble the next two rules. This formulation may be less misleading than "Do not disable" because disabling a person might be thought to require causing a loss of ability that makes a person count as disabled in that respect. However, if a person had some exceptional physical or mental abilities and was deprived of those abilities, that would count as a violation of this rule even if the person did not count as disabled in any respect. Nevertheless, since the present formulation, like the formulation of the rule "Do not kill," seems to have sufficiently more rhetorical force than its slightly more precise alternative, it seems worth keeping.

Blinding a person or cutting off an arm or a leg is obviously a violation of this rule. Keeping a person permanently blindfolded or tying up his arms or legs so that they cannot be used seems to fit better as a violation of the following rule, "Do not deprive of freedom," rather than as a violation of this rule. When you are no longer able to do something that previously you could do, and this is the result of some action by another person, the way things were before the violation determines which rule was violated. If the action of the other person changed you, then it should be regarded as a violation of the rule that prohibits disabling. If the action of the other person changed your environment, then it should be regarded as a violation of the rule that prohibits depriving of freedom. It is more important that every immoral act be covered by some moral rule than it is to determine which particular rule is violated.

This rule prohibits causing the loss not only of any physical ability but also of any mental or volitional ability.[14] Although physically disabling a person is the most common kind of disabling, it is not uncommon for persons to be harmed by causing them to be mentally or volitionally disabled. Some drugs can cause a loss of mental abilities such as the ability to remember or to calculate. Putting persons in some extreme environments may cause volitional disabilities such as compulsions or phobias, and giving them drugs, including alcohol or cigarettes, may result in their developing addictions, another kind of volitional disability. Intentionally doing anything to a person in order to take away his ability to do any kind of action is a violation of the rule that prohibits disabling him. Preventing persons from exercising an ability for long enough may result in their losing that ability, so that some violations of the rule prohibiting the depriving of freedom may also result in a violation of this rule.

Of course, that a person suffers a loss of ability does not mean that someone violated this rule. Animals can cause disabilities and some abilities naturally diminish with age. Accidents, including sports injuries, often result in disabilities, and even when another person is involved, no one may have violated the rule prohibiting disabling. As with the other moral rules, intentionally causing or intending to cause a loss of ability is always a violation. However, determining whether unintentionally acting in a way that results in a loss of ability counts as a violation of the rule depends on the interpretation of the rule in that society. Also, as with all the other rules, violations of this rule may be justified. With their patients' valid consent, doctors often justifiably violate this rule, for example, amputate a leg in order to prevent a patient's death.

4. "Do not deprive of freedom."

The rule prohibiting the deprivation of freedom must be taken to prohibit doing something to a person without consent as well as depriving her of opportunities and resources. However, to interpret this rule as including all prohibitions on doing anything that makes persons no longer able to do something that they used to be able to do would make this rule prohibit too much. Normally, this rule is not interpreted as prohibiting my freedom to restrict the freedom of others to make use of some items to which the law gives me ownership. As explained in the discussion of the previous rule, violations of this rule are actions that make a person unable to do something by altering his environment or situation, rather than by altering the person himself. The clearest case of depriving a person of freedom involves putting him in prison. Any physical barriers to a person's movements such as tying him up with rope or chains or locking him in a room count as depriving him of his freedom. Serious threats also count as depriving of freedom, so that coercion can be taken as depriving of freedom. It is the threat of punishment that makes it appropriate to say that the criminal law deprives people of their freedom to do certain kinds of actions. However, most criminal laws that prohibit violations of the moral rules are justified deprivations of freedom.

Job discrimination against qualified people of a particular race, religion, or ethnic background counts as a violation of this rule. However, people would not normally interpret the rule so that it counts as depriving a person of an opportunity if another, more qualified person is hired for the job. Except for intentional deprivations of freedom, determining when this rule is violated is more difficult than determining when any of the other rules are being violated. When many people are competing for a job or entrance to a college or university, it is often difficult to know how to determine whether the person was deprived of an opportunity or simply lost the competition. Someone who wins a race fairly does not thereby deprive the person who came in second of the opportunity to receive the gold medal.

Even when there is no competition, not every action by a person that results in someone not getting what she would have received if not for that action counts as depriving her of opportunity. If a person has been waiting in line to attend a popular concert and buys the last two tickets, he has not thereby violated the rule "Do not deprive of freedom" with regard to all the people behind him in line. If he takes the last parking space, he has not violated this rule with regard to the person in the car behind him, unless he has done something inappropriate to get in front of that person. It is important to note that he has not violated the rule at all; it is not that he has violated the rule but has an adequate justification or legitimate excuse. If he does not intentionally plan to deprive someone of the opportunity to buy a ticket to the concert or park her car, then, if he has not violated any other moral rule such as breaking the law, he has not violated the rule against depriving of freedom. This is true even if he knows that what he is doing will result in the other person not being able to buy a ticket or park her car.

It is a difficult matter to decide when an action that results in another person not having an opportunity she would have had if not for your action violates the rule against depriving of freedom. It is the same problem that arose in the discussion of when an action that results in another person suffering unpleasant feelings that she would not have suffered if not for your action counts as your breaking the rule "Do not cause pain." As the examples in the previous paragraph show, when your action results in another person not having an opportunity, whether you have broken the rule prohibiting the deprivation of freedom is not decided by engaging in a scientific analysis of what caused the loss of freedom the other person would have had if not for your action. Rather, those who think that you need a justification or excuse for doing what you did regard you as having broken the rule and consequently as having caused the loss of freedom; those who think you do not need a justification or excuse do not regard you as having broken the rule.

Actions that change a person's environment or situation so that she is not able to do something that she could do without that change may count as depriving a person of freedom. Thus, intentionally taking away resources may count as breaking this rule. Stealing money is not only a violation of the rule that prohibits breaking the law but also a violation of this rule. It also counts as depriving a person of freedom if you have a duty to provide that person with the resources to do something and you do not do so. The standard case of depriving people of freedom, such as locking them in a cell, involves taking away their opportunity to do very many things. However, it also counts as a violation of this rule to deprive a person of a single opportunity, such as the opportunity to participate in some activity such as a school play.

This rule not only prohibits depriving persons of the freedom to act but also prohibits depriving them of the freedom from being acted upon. Intentionally touching a person whom one has good reason to believe does not want to be touched counts as violating her freedom, so that a man's intentional bumping into a woman on a crowded subway is a violation of this rule. However, his unintentional bumping into her is not. In some circumstances, listening to or looking at a person without their knowledge might count as a violation of this rule. It might be held that a person's freedom to be unobserved is being taken away. Societies can differ in what they count as invasions of privacy. Giving a person a pill or any other medication without her consent also counts as violating her freedom. Some of these violations may be justified. But whether medicating a mentally ill person who might otherwise seriously harm herself is justified or not, it still counts as depriving that person of her freedom. This kind of violation of a person's freedom is significantly different from depriving her of the freedom to act. However, we normally talk about such actions as depriving a person of her freedom. Thus, including this kind of action as a violation of the rule against depriving a person of freedom seems both appropriate and easily understood.

5. "Do not deprive of pleasure."

People feel pleasure when they desire to continue doing or experiencing what they are presently doing or experiencing. Eating an ice cream cone, having your back scratched, working on a crossword puzzle, all provide pleasure when, even without external motivation, people want to continue these activities or experiences. Similarly, when, without independent motivation, people no longer want these activities or experiences to continue, they are no longer getting pleasure from them. People can be deprived of pleasure by preventing them from continuing to do or experience what they are presently doing or experiencing. Normally, to stop scratching a person's back does not count as violating this rule, but taking away a person's ice cream cone does. Again, apart from intentional violations, when your action results in another person not having some pleasure she would have had if not for your action, whether your action is considered a violation of this rule is determined by whether you are thought to need a justification or excuse.

Many would view this rule as unnecessary. It might be thought that any depriving of pleasure would necessarily cause unpleasant feelings and hence be covered by the rule prohibiting causing pain. Although it is quite likely that depriving of pleasure normally involves causing unpleasant feelings, it does not seem that this is always true. Talking loudly at a concert deprives people of the pleasure of hearing the music even if it does not also make them upset, which it usually does. On a much more serious level, female circumcision, even when it does not involve causing pain, which it normally does, would still need to be justified, for it is intended to deprive the girl of a significant amount of sexual pleasure in the future.

Just as the rule prohibiting the deprivation of freedom could be interpreted so as to include all actions that are prohibited by the rule "Do not disable," so it could also be interpreted to include all actions that are prohibited by this rule. Destroying any beautiful object could be taken as violating either this rule or the previous one. Depriving of sources of pleasure might be taken as depriving of the opportunity to experience pleasure. The point of formulating these rules is to make explicit the system that accounts for all of our moral judgments about what is morally prohibited or required. It is not a problem if an act can be considered as a violation of more than one rule. What is important is that all acts that are normally considered to be immoral are covered by at least one of these rules.

Summary of the first five rules

The first five rules prohibit causing all of the basic harms. These harms are (1) death or permanent loss of consciousness; (2) pain, including all unpleasant feelings such as displeasure (anger), disgust, anxiety (fear), and sadness, as well as physical and emotional pain; (3) disability, including the loss of any physical, mental, or volitional ability; (4) loss of freedom, which includes loss of opportunity and resources and also loss of bodily integrity and privacy; and (5) loss of pleasure, including the loss of that which provides pleasure. Apart from death, each of these harms includes many subcategories, so that everything that is normally considered a basic harm or evil is included in this list. Two facts support this claim to completeness. First, nothing counts as a punishment unless it involves the infliction of one of these harms. Second, nothing counts as a malady, that is, as a disease or injury, unless it involves one or more of these basic harms.

6. "Do not deceive."

This formulation of the rule is preferable to the more familiar formulation "Do not lie" because intending to deceive by making a false statement, which is what lying is, is only one way of intentionally deceiving. Intentionally deceiving someone in a nonverbal way is as much a violation of this rule as lying. The positive formulation, "Tell the truth," if taken literally, requires too much, prohibiting a person from refusing to talk. This means that it prohibits withholding information. However, people are generally not morally required to tell a person something they know, not even something that the other person might want to know. Of course, if a person has a duty to provide some information, such as a doctor having a duty to provide information to a patient about his diagnosis and prognosis, then withholding that information does count as deceiving.

As with the first five rules, not only intentional attempts to deceive, whether successful or not, count as violations of this rule, but also some unintended causing of persons to have false beliefs may also count as violations. If a person knows or should know that certain kinds of behavior, such as repeating rumors that he has no reason to believe to be true, will significantly increase the probability that people will have false beliefs, then repeating those rumors can be taken as violating this rule. Any behavior that a person knows or should know will significantly increase the chances that someone will have false beliefs can count as violating this rule. However, behavior that involves your personal appearance, such as coloring your hair, is not interpreted as violating the rule that prohibits deceiving, without even considering the intention. Requiring people to justify this kind of behavior would have worse consequences than allowing them to do as they please.

Some regard false beliefs as an additional basic harm; however, unless false beliefs significantly increase the chances of someone suffering one of the previously listed harms, a rational person need not be concerned about having them. Of course, false beliefs so often do significantly increase a person's chances of suffering one of the basic harms (or decrease his chances of gaining a basic good) that it does not make much difference whether false beliefs are considered a basic harm. Deceiving always needs some excuse or justification in order not to be morally wrong. Further, even if individual acts of deception may not cause any significant increase in a person's chances of suffering one of the basic harms, widespread deception always significantly increases people's chances of suffering the basic harms. That individual violations may sometimes cause no harm is what differentiates the second five rules from the first five. Surprisingly, widespread violation of the rule "Do not deceive" may cause more serious harm than similarly widespread violations of some of the first five rules.

7. "Keep your promises."

This rule differs from all of the previous rules in that it is formulated as a requirement rather than as a prohibition. However, if this rule were formulated as "Do not break your promises," it would make no practical difference. What differentiates this rule from the previous six and enables it to be phrased positively is that it presupposes that a person has already done something, that is, made a promise. Given this fact, there is no practical difference between saying "Keep your promises" and "Do not break your promises." None of the previous rules presupposes any prior contact between people. The first six rules can be violated with regard to a complete stranger, someone with whom you have had no previous contact. This rule cannot be violated with regard to a complete stranger, for you must have made a promise to that person before this rule applies. However, all moral agents will have made some promises, so that this rule has as wide an application as the first six.

This rule prohibits breaking both formal promises such as contracts and informal promises where you simply state to someone your intention to do something. When you do the latter and know that your statement of intention will lead the person to whom it is given to count on your doing that thing, your statement of intention is a promise. The performative utterance "I promise" evolved in order to make explicit to the person to whom you stated your intention that she could count on your doing what you said you would do.[15] However, circumstances often make it unnecessary to say, "I promise," in order to make a promise. Promising when you do not intend to do what you promised is itself a violation of the previous rule prohibiting deception, but if one then does not keep the promise, this rule is also violated. Violations of this rule, however, need not be violations of the rule prohibiting deception, for broken promises are often made by people who intend to keep them when they make them.

Kant seems to hold that one should never make a lying promise, but it is not difficult to imagine circumstances that would provide an adequate justification for doing so. If someone threatens to seriously harm your family if you do not promise to do something for him, you are completely justified in making that promise with no intention of keeping it if you can arrange to break the promise without compromising their safety. There are also many cases, some discussed by Plato (*Republic* 3.3.1c), in which a person made a promise with the intention of keeping it, but circumstances changed sufficiently that the promise should not be kept. Nonetheless, one generally needs a reason for breaking a promise, for widespread violation of this rule leads to an enormous increase in the amount of harm suffered and especially in the amount of benefits lost.

This rule is often broken unintentionally. At the time of making the promise, the person does intend to keep it, but either simply forgets about it or something comes up which conflicts with keeping the promise. Although there may be an explanation for a person's forgetting a promise that provides a legitimate excuse for his failing to keep his promise, this explanation cannot justify his failing to keep it. To justify a violation of a rule is to advocate that the rule be violated, that is, to claim that there is an adequate reason for violating it; to excuse a violation is only to advocate that the person not be blamed for the violation. This distinction between justification and excuse applies to all of the rules. If I break a promise to meet you for dinner in order to take a seriously injured person to the hospital, I am justified in breaking that promise.

If I break the same promise because my car broke down and I had no way to get to dinner, I have an excuse.

8. "Do not cheat."

Cheating is an interesting concept, so it is quite surprising that there are hardly any philosophical discussions of it. Partly this is due to the mistaken view that cheating, like lying, is simply a subclass of deceiving, or else that cheating is simply some kind of promise breaking. The case of a boss who openly cheats when he plays golf with his subordinates because he knows that they will not protest shows conclusively that cheating does not require deception. Cheating normally does involve deception because most cases of cheating occur between equals. The cheater knows that the others participating in the game or other voluntary activity (i.e., an activity in which persons participate voluntarily) will not allow him to gain the advantages of cheating.

In the example of the boss who regularly cheats while playing golf with his subordinates, no promise, explicit or implicit, to follow the rules has been made to the subordinates. Although closely related to deceiving or breaking a promise, cheating is a distinct kind of behavior. The paradigm of cheating is violating the rules of a game in order to gain some advantage over others participating in that game, and usually there are no explicit penalties for such a violation except expulsion from the game. When a violation of the rules becomes accepted as a part of the game and explicit penalties are attached to the violation, such as a foul in basketball, that violation is no longer considered to be cheating. It is often done quite openly, and all playing the game regard it as legitimate.

That cheating involves violating the rules of a game explains why it is so natural to talk about cheating at solitaire, even though it is obvious that no deception or broken promise is involved. However, the moral rules always concern our behavior toward others, and because cheating at solitaire does not involve anyone else, it is not a moral matter. If no one else is affected and you do not have an adequate reason for acting, it is not immoral but irrational to kill yourself, cause yourself pain, disable yourself, or deprive yourself of freedom or pleasure. Similarly, it is also not a moral matter to deceive yourself or break a promise to yourself. All of the moral rules are to be understood as prohibiting or requiring behavior that affects others, directly or indirectly.

Games are the best examples of voluntary activities in which cheating occurs. Usually no one playing the game is in a position like that of the boss who plays with his subordinates, and so all are expected to abide by the rules. Cheating on exams or papers is also prohibited by this rule, even though such cheating, when done in the context of an honor code, is also the violation of a promise to abide by the rules of the school. Even if cheating becomes common enough that explicit penalties short of expulsion are attached for cheating, it still counts as cheating. This is because it is still an expectation of the activity that students will not cheat, and successful cheating results in the cheater gaining some advantage over others participating in that activity.

Cheating also occurs in business transactions, as when a grocer puts his thumb on the scale when weighing some item that is sold by weight. Such actions are also prohibited by the law; nonetheless, this kind of activity so closely resembles the paradigm cases of cheating that it continues to be regarded as cheating and is prohibited by this rule. The same is true of cheating on one's income tax, even though there are explicit legal penalties for doing so. What is common to all of these cases, including cheating on an exam, is that the cheater is gaining an advantage over other people participating in that activity, such as those taking the exam, by violating the rules that everyone is expected to follow. If students came to realize that, because grades and standing in class are comparative, someone cheating on an exam or paper disadvantages them, not the school or the teacher, there might be less acceptance of academic cheating by students than there now seems to be.

Cheating is the basic way of acting unfairly. Even what we call unfair games, such as playing with marked cards or loaded dice, involve some people violating the rules of an activity in order to gain an advantage over the other participants. Unlike the previous moral rules, it may seem that there is no adequate justification for cheating. However, this is false. If someone threatens to kill your family if he wins the game, you are completely justified in cheating in order to win. If he threatens to kill your family if he loses, it is not cheating to let him win, for cheating involves violating the rules in order to gain an advantage in the activity. Nonetheless, throwing a fight or a game in order to gain some advantage outside the game, such as making money by betting against yourself or your team, also counts as a violation of this rule. In the basic sense of the word "unfair," only the violation of this moral rule counts as unfair. Unfortunately, "unfair" is now commonly used simply as a synonym for "immoral."

The one respect in which this rule seems to differ from all of the other rules is that it does not seem possible to violate this rule unintentionally. If a person breaks the rules unintentionally or unknowingly, then he is usually not said to be cheating. However, if he later realizes that he has broken a rule of the game, not reporting this would be a violation of this rule. This rule may even be taken to prohibit participating in an activity without knowing the rules when everyone participating in that activity is expected to know them.

9. *"Obey the law."*

Concentration on an extremely small number of immoral laws, such as laws supporting racial discrimination or segregation, has led some to think that this rule could not be a moral rule. But this same kind of reasoning could be used to show that "Keep your promises" is not a moral rule, for there are many immoral promises. This kind of consideration does not show that "Obey the law" and "Keep your promises" are not moral rules, for to claim that a rule is a moral rule only means that violating it without an adequate justification is acting immorally. That a law or a promise is immoral usually provides an adequate justification for breaking the rule. However, if all that is known about an action is that it is a violation of the law, then a justification is needed.

Furthermore, most laws are good laws; that is, they help the society to function successfully. Traffic laws are paradigm examples of such laws, as are tax laws. Without such laws modern society would not function. There might be better traffic laws or tax laws than the laws a particular society has, but unless those laws are unbelievably bad, less harm is suffered if everyone obeys the law rather than acting according to what they believe would be better laws. This is Hobbes's powerful argument for obeying the sovereign, which means obeying the laws of the society. Except for morally unjustifiable laws, less harm results if everyone follows the same set of rules governing their interactions than if each person follows his own set of rules. This is true even if their own set of rules would make the society function better if that set were the laws instead of the laws now in place. When the laws are very bad, there will always be an adequate justification for violating them.

For the purpose of this rule, a law is defined as follows: *A law is a rule that is part of a system (the legal system). The existence of that system is known to all moral agents in the society to which it applies, and that system directly or indirectly significantly influences their behavior. Some of these rules apply to members of that society independently of their wish to be subject to them, and some of them have explicit penalties for violation.* That the legal system is known to all moral agents does not mean that all of them know every law in the system, and not even every law that applies to them. No citizen of any large society knows every law, but all know there is a legal system and they know many of the rules of that system, especially those that apply to them. Legal systems, unlike the moral system, are usually formal systems in that they have procedures for resolving disagreements and arriving at unique answers to controversial questions. These procedures usually involve authorities, such as judges, who are responsible for providing the unique answer.

Because legal systems of small, isolated societies may not have explicit procedures and authorities, some people falsely consider them to be moral systems. However, legal systems, even legal systems of small, isolated societies, differ from the moral system in important ways. One way is that the legal system contains a procedure that can resolve all disagreements, whereas the common moral system does not. A far more important difference is that people can be held legally responsible for their actions even if they are completely legitimately ignorant that they are violating a law. This is true for those quasi-religious legal systems in which some laws involve taboos, as well as for the strict liability laws of the most sophisticated modern legal systems. However, no one is held morally responsible for their actions if they are completely legitimately ignorant that they are violating a moral rule, including the rule prohibiting violating the law. Another important difference is that even when it would be irrational to obey a law, there might be no adequate legal justification for not obeying it. However, whenever it would be irrational to obey a moral rule, there is always an adequate moral justification for not obeying it. It is never irrational to use the moral system as a guide, whereas it may sometimes be irrational to use the legal system as a guide.

All legal systems prohibit morally unjustified killing and other morally unjustified serious harming of people as well as many serious cases of deceiving, breaking promises, and cheating. However, the laws prohibiting these kinds of actions are, as indicated above, not identical to the moral rules prohibiting the same kinds of actions. Even if, in a given society, there were no laws prohibiting any of these kinds of actions, it would still be immoral to do them without adequate justification. Some actions, however, would not be immoral if there were no law prohibiting that kind of action. For example, no other moral rule need be violated by marrying more than one person at a time, but if a society has a well-known law prohibiting bigamy or polygamy, it is immoral in that society to marry more than one person unless one has an adequate justification.

Living in a society has many similarities to participating in a voluntary activity, and breaking the law has many similarities to cheating. Indeed, violating the tax laws is often called cheating on your taxes. Those who pay their taxes are being taken advantage of by those who do not pay. The fewer restrictions there are on a person leaving a society, the more that living in a society is like participating in a voluntary activity and the greater the similarity between cheating and breaking the law. Of course, there are differences, but the similarities are significant. Participants in voluntary activities justifiably depend upon other participants to abide by the rules of that activity. People living in a society justifiably depend upon other people living in that society to abide by the laws of that society. Any significant increase in unjustified breaking of the law increases the probability that people in that society will suffer greater harms. Just imagine what it would be like if people could not depend on other people to stop at a red light.

10. "Do your duty."

The rule requiring a person to do his duty requires doing those actions that are a person's duty because of a special role, such as being a doctor, lawyer, parent, or teacher. It also requires doing those duties that arise from circumstances, such as helping someone in great need when one is in a unique or close-to-unique position to provide that help and can do so at little cost. Like the previous three rules, this rule presupposes that people are living in a society with all sorts of interactions between its members. All societies have a practice of promising; they all have some games and other voluntary activities in which there are established goals and standards or rules that everyone participating in the activity is expected to abide by; and they all have some legal system for guiding conduct and settling disputes. They also have roles in which those occupying the roles are required to do various kinds of actions. Some roles, such as that of parent, are often determined biologically but may come about in several other ways, such as adoption. Other roles are the result of paid employment, such as those of doctors, nurses, police, and teachers. Such duties are not limited to requirements to do specific things, as a night watchman must make his rounds; often there is a duty to do things in a specified way. A judge must not only show up for trial but must also make her decisions impartially. Most roles have duties, more or less precise, attached to them.

People who do not fulfill their duties and do not have an adequate justification for neglecting them are regarded as acting immorally. The term "duty" has taken on a moral connotation, so that no one can have a duty to do what is immoral. That means that a person does not have a duty to do whatever he is paid to do. A driver of a getaway car may have been paid to wait for and then help those robbing a bank to escape, but it would be incorrect to say that he has a duty to do those jobs. If it is immoral for people working in an advertising agency to try to sell harmful, addictive drugs, they are not correct in claiming that they have a duty to do so because it is what they are getting paid to do.

If a person has a job that requires deceiving, for example, engaging in false advertising, such that no fully informed rational person would favor everyone knowing that deceiving is allowed in these circumstances, that is, publicly allow it, such deceiving is unjustified and hence immoral. A person cannot have a duty to do it. However, if a person has a job that requires deceiving, for example, deceiving to protect a company's legitimate secrets, such that some fully informed rational persons would publicly allow such deceiving while others would not, both deceiving and not deceiving are weakly justified in these circumstances. In this situation, a person may have a duty to deceive and it is not immoral to do so. If a person has a job that requires deceiving, for example, engaging in undercover police work to prevent a terrorist attack, such that all fully informed rational persons would publicly allow deceiving, it is strongly justified to deceive, and not deceiving when it is your duty to deceive is unjustified and immoral. Weakly justified violations are, by definition, the kinds of violations about whose justification equally informed rational persons disagree, so it is possible for some duties to be controversial.

Not only are there limitations to what activities can be duties, there are also duties that are not tied to any particular role but are the result of circumstances. These duties need not even be part of the structure of a particular society but are duties that everyone in those circumstances has. There is general agreement that a person has such a duty to help when (1) she is in physical proximity to someone in need of help to avoid a serious harm such as death or permanent disability; (2) she is in a unique or close-to-unique position to provide that help; and (3) it would be relatively cost free for her to provide that help.[16]

Some people, including some philosophers, claim that there are duties to help when (1), (2), and even (3), are not true. They claim that any time a person can prevent any harm, not only serious harms, without anyone suffering comparable harms, she has a duty to do so. Although this position has significant initial rhetorical force, it has serious problems if taken literally. Almost everyone who can afford luxuries sometimes buys them, even though that money could always prevent serious evils for other people. If the unrestricted formulation of the duty to help were actually a duty, then spending money on luxuries for yourself or your children or for nice gifts for friends would always be acting immorally. Even worse, on this view it is immoral for a person to relax for any time beyond what is necessary for maintenance of physical or mental health when he could be preventing serious harm to others.

Although both Kant and Mill claim that we do have an un-restricted duty to help, it is what they call a "duty of imperfect obligation," which is not what many, including me, would nor-mally call a duty at all.[17] Kant and Mill agree that people are not morally required to fulfill duties of imperfect obligation whenever they apply, in contrast to what they call a "duty of perfect obli-gation" and duties in the common sense of the term.[18] It is true that everyone morally ought to help those in need, even those with whom one has no relationship, when it can be done at a relatively insignificant cost, but this does not mean there is a duty to do so. It means only that all moral agents would encourage helping those in need when it can be done at a relatively insignificant cost and may even criticize those who do not do so. However, this is far less demanding than saying that everyone has a duty to help those in need when that can be done at a relatively insignificant cost. To regard helping everyone in need, even when that involves only a relatively insignificant cost, as a moral requirement is to favor making people who do not do so liable to punishment.

Philosophers also often use the term "duty" as a synonym for "moral requirement" and claim that all moral agents have a duty to keep their promises, as well as a duty not to kill. In ordinary usage, "duty" is not used in this very wide sense but is restricted to moral requirements that stem from a social role or job or from being in some special circumstances. The duty to help is a duty of the latter sort. Although there may be particular duties to help, common morality does not regard the unrestricted formulation of the duty to help as a genuine duty or a moral requirement. There is not even a social role that requires following the unrestricted formulation of the duty to help. Unless a person has a social role that requires helping some others, a person has a duty to help only when helping can be done at a relatively insignificant cost, he is in physical proximity to the person in need of help to avoid serious harm, and he is in a unique or close-to-unique position to provide that help.

⠿
Violations of Moral Rules Involve Liability to Punishment

Common morality distinguishes between what is morally required and what is morally encouraged. To regard a kind of action as morally required is to favor making a person liable to punishment for any serious instance of a failure to do that kind of action. Similarly, to regard a kind of action as morally prohibited is to favor making a person liable to punishment for any serious instance of doing the prohibited action. Punishment involves inflicting an evil on someone who has violated a rule by a person who has a duty to inflict that evil. To hold that a person should be liable to punishment for some action or omission means favoring giving someone authority to decide whether to inflict an evil on a person for that action or omission. According to common morality, unless there are adequate reasons for not doing so (e.g., the harms caused by government intrusion in order to punish violations between private persons outweigh the benefits of deterring such violations), all serious unjustified violations of moral rules should be prohibited by laws or subject to a legal suit by the individual harmed. I count as punishment any harms inflicted by the legal system, both harms inflicted as the result of being found guilty of violating a law and the harms suffered due to a successful legal action by an individual against a person who has caused her to suffer any serious harm because that person violated a moral rule with regard to her.

All persons are morally required to obey the moral rules unless they have an adequate justification for violating the rule. However, unless they have a duty to do so, no one is morally required to help people. This does not mean that people cannot be criticized for not giving to worthy charities when they have far more money than they need; it means only that people should not be liable to punishment for failing to give to charities. Rational persons are justifiably reluctant to give authority to any government to punish a person simply for failing to act on a moral ideal.

All serious unjustified violations of moral rules should make a person liable to punishment. However, it is not quite so clear that violations that are only weakly justified should make one liable to punishment as well. But if liability to punishment were not allowed when people disagree about whether the violation of the law is justified, then the stability of the state would be impossible to maintain. As shown by judges who praise the moral character of those whom they punish for engaging in morally justifiable civil disobedience, common morality accepts the seeming paradox that it may be morally justified to punish weakly justified violations of the moral rules. This is a natural consequence of common morality's recognition that people sometimes disagree about whether a violation of a moral rule should be allowed. Only when all moral agents favor everyone knowing that they are allowed to violate the rule in these same circumstances, that is, when it is a strongly justified violation, does common morality hold that a violation of a moral rule should not make one liable to punishment.

Of course, favoring liability to punishment does not mean that everyone agrees that all unjustified and weakly justified violations of a moral rule should be punished. Punishing trivial violations would probably cause more harm than it prevents, and it is likely that punishing some significant violations would have the same effect. However, any significant violation of a moral rule when that violation is not strongly justified is like entering a negative lottery. Consequences that a person did not intend or foresee, perhaps even consequences that were not foreseeable (e.g., a person dying during the commission of a burglary), may affect his liability to punishment. Common morality acknowledges that no one is subject to moral judgments for consequences that were unforeseeable. However, once a person enters the punishment lottery by a violation of a moral rule that is not strongly justified, common morality holds that how much punishment he receives is often legally determined by factors outside the person's control.

::
Justifying Violations of the Moral Rules

There is universal agreement about those kinds of actions that count as immoral unless one has an adequate justification for doing them, or, as I have been expressing it, about what rules are moral rules. My concern here is with the procedure for deciding whether a violation is justified when there is agreement about the interpretation of a moral rule and about who is protected by morality. I am concerned with the justification of a clear violation of a moral rule with regard to a moral agent, someone who is regarded by everyone as fully protected by morality. No one has any serious doubts that killing, causing pain or disability, depriving of freedom or pleasure, deceiving, breaking promises, cheating, breaking the law, and neglecting a duty need justification in order not to be immoral. But sometimes there are serious disagreements about what counts as an adequate justification.

Kant seems to hold that it is never justified to break some of these rules (*On a Supposed Right to Lie because of Philanthropic Concerns*).[19] A well-known example is his claim that it is morally wrong for a person to lie to a hired killer in order to protect an innocent person from being killed by that hired killer. This view is regarded, even by his defenders, as a serious mistake. Moral agents agree that some violations of the moral rules are justified. Even killing may be justified if it is done in self-defense.

Mill seems to hold that there is an adequate justification for breaking any rule whenever the overall consequences of breaking that rule would be better than the overall consequences of obeying it.[20] Mill insists that when taking into account the consequences of violating the rule, it is important to give the appropriate weight to the possible weakening of the rule. Nonetheless, in a particular situation, his view entails that it is only the consequences, direct and indirect, of the particular act that are decisive in determining whether the violation is justified. This view yields an incorrect answer to the question about whether it is morally acceptable for a pre-med student to cheat on an exam when (1) the exam is on the honor principle, making it virtually certain that he will not be caught; (2) no other student will be harmed because both the course and the exam are graded as pass/fail; (3) knowing the material is not essential for his future career because the exam is in a course in metaphysics; and (4) there are the standard financial and emotional consequences for the student and his parents if he flunks the exam and course.

Common morality incorporates a more complex account of the justification of a violation of a moral rule. It incorporates the kind of impartiality that Kant is mistakenly regarded as having provided by the Categorical Imperative.[21] It also incorporates a concern with consequences, but unlike in Mill's formulation, these are not limited to the consequences of the particular action. Common morality differs from both Mill and Kant in another very important respect. Indeed, common morality differs from most philosophical descriptions of morality in this respect, because it holds that equally informed, impartial, rational persons sometimes can disagree about whether a violation of a moral rule should be allowed.

When every qualified person, that is, an impartial rational person who knows all the morally relevant features of the violation, agrees that a particular violation should be allowed, then that violation is strongly justified and a person should not be liable to punishment for violating the rule. When every qualified person agrees that the violation should not be allowed, then the violation is unjustified and a person should be liable to punishment for violating the rule. When people disagree about whether the violation should be allowed, the violation is weakly justified, but a person still should be liable to punishment for violating the rule. Common morality acknowledges that punishment for a weakly justified violation may be morally justified. Recognizing that equally informed, impartial, rational persons can disagree about whether a given violation of a moral rule should be allowed makes it understandable why weakly justified civil disobedience may be justifiably punished.

::

The Two-Step Procedure for Justifying Violations of the Moral Rules

The first step: Using the morally relevant features to describe the act

The first step of the two-step procedure for justifying a violation of a moral rule involves finding out all the relevant facts. Everyone recognizes that circumstances alter cases, that a change in the facts can change whether a violation of a moral rule is justified. But not all facts are relevant. It is normally not relevant what day of the week it is or what time of day or where the violation takes place. Thus, before one can find out all the relevant facts, it is necessary to determine which facts are relevant. Common morality must be understandable to all moral agents; therefore, all of the relevant facts must be describable in a way that all moral agents understand. The function of the morally relevant features is to provide a complete morally relevant description of the action.

A morally relevant feature of a moral rule violation is a fact such that if it were different it could affect whether some rational person would hold that everyone should know that a violation with this feature is allowed, that is, should be publicly allowed. If all of these features are the same for two violations, then they are the same kind of violation. A person who favors everyone knowing that one violation with these features is allowed must also favor everyone knowing that another violation with these same features is allowed, even if the first is done by a friend and the second is done by a stranger. It does not follow that two different people who regard a violation as of the same kind must both make the same moral judgment about the violation. Equally informed, impartial, rational people may sometimes disagree in their judgments about whether to favor everyone knowing that a violation with these features is allowed. These disagreements can result from differences in their estimates of the harms and benefits that would occur if everyone knew that this kind of violation was allowed, versus their estimates of the harms and benefits that would occur if everyone knew that this kind of violation was not allowed, or from their differences in their rankings of these harms and benefits.

Those facts that common morality takes as relevant can be categorized as answers to the following ten questions. Those facts that are answers to the following questions are morally relevant; they are the morally relevant features of the act or the morally relevant circumstances. Although there is no doubt that all of the listed features are morally relevant and that this list includes all of the most important morally relevant features, there might be further features that are morally relevant. But all of these features must be describable in a way that all moral agents can understand. This list of features is derived from noting the kinds of facts that can change the moral decisions and judgments of impartial rational persons; it is not derived from some a priori moral or philosophical principle.

1. Which moral rule is being violated?

It is clear that stronger reasons are needed for violating the rule "Do not kill" than for the rule "Do not deprive of pleasure." What may not be so obvious is that, even when the consequences of the particular act are worse, it may be justified to cause some unpleasant feelings when it would not be justified to deceive. For example, when the probability of success is the same, it may be justified to harass a patient into continuing a treatment that it is irrational for him to refuse, whereas in the same circumstances it would not be justified to deceive that patient. This is because even when violations of the two different rules are the same in all of their other morally relevant features, the consequences of everyone knowing that a violation of the rule prohibiting deception is allowed may be far worse than everyone knowing that a violation of the rule prohibiting causing unpleasant feelings is allowed.

2. Which evils or harms (including their kind, severity, probability, the length of time they will be suffered, and their distribution) are being (a) caused by the violation, (b) avoided (not caused) by the violation, or (c) prevented by the violation?

This feature resembles the calculus that Bentham provided for determining whether an act was morally right or wrong, except that it includes only harms (which Bentham limited to pains), not benefits (which Bentham limited to pleasures). The recognition that there are different kinds of evils, such as death, pain (and even kinds of pain), and so on, does not prevent genuine agreement on the facts. Even though persons may rank these harms differently, this should not affect their description of the kind of violation. The ranking of the harms plays its role only in the second step of the procedure when considering whether to favor everyone knowing that this kind of violation is allowed.

Even if two people agree on what harms (evils) will be caused, avoided, or prevented by a particular act, and on the benefits (goods) being promoted (see feature 5), and on the alternatives that are available (see feature 8), they still may not agree on what kind of act it is. No one doubts that the evils being caused, avoided, and prevented and that the goods being promoted are morally relevant. However, there are other morally relevant features in addition to these consequences, including the feature already mentioned, the moral rule that is being broken. The claim that only consequences are morally relevant results in many counterintuitive moral judgments. Whether a person is violating a moral rule—for example, deceiving or breaking a promise—is morally relevant. Even if all of the consequences of two acts, one involving a violation of a moral rule and the other not, are the same, one act may be morally acceptable and the other not.

Although their views have no practical consequences, some philosophers claim, counterintuitively, that actual consequences, even if unforeseeable, are relevant to a moral judgment about an action—as if a meteor falling on a playground months after it was built is relevant to any moral judgment about having built the playground there. Other philosophers claim to hold that only intended consequences have relevance to moral decisions and judgments. Contrary to both of these views, it is the consequences foreseen by the agent that are most relevant to the making of moral decisions, and foreseeable goods and evils that are most relevant to the making of moral judgments.

It is morally relevant whether a person is causing some harm intentionally or only doing so knowingly (see feature 9). However, moral judgments are correctly made not only about actions with known, though unintended consequences but even about actions with consequences unknown to the agent, if he should have known about them. Actual consequences that were unforeseeable at the time of acting play no role in moral judgments, although they may appropriately be considered in determining the punishment of a person who commits an unjustifiable or weakly justifiable violation of a moral rule.[22]

What counts as foreseen and intended consequences is completely determined by what the agent foresees and intends, whereas the agent has no special status at all in determining the actual consequences. Foreseeable consequences are neither completely determined by the agent nor are they completely unrelated to the agent. Foreseeable consequences are determined by the beliefs, knowledge, and intelligence of the agent; they are what she can be expected to foresee. What a significant number of people with similar beliefs, knowledge, and intelligence would foresee in a situation is foreseeable. Foreseeable consequences are agent relative, which is made clear by the fact that two people can cooperate in performing the same action and yet some of the consequences of that action are foreseeable to one of them and unforeseeable to the other. Even though foreseeable consequences are relative to the beliefs, knowledge, and intelligence of the agent, they are still objective factors.

It is foreseeable to a normal adult that playing with matches can cause a serious fire. This is not foreseeable to a normal three-year-old. A significant number of people with the beliefs, knowledge, and intelligence of a normal adult would foresee the consequences of playing with matches. It is not the case that a significant number of people with the beliefs, knowledge, and intelligence of a normal three-year-old would foresee this. Persons can, within limits, disagree about whether the consequences of an action were foreseeable to the agent. It is often important to decide this, for if they were, he is not excused, and if they were not, he is.

3. What are the desires and beliefs of the person toward whom the rule is being violated?

(a) WHAT ARE THE DESIRES OF THE PERSON TOWARD WHOM THE RULE IS BEING VIOLATED?   There are several possibilities. (1) The person has a rational desire that results in his wanting the rule to be violated. For example, a patient desires to live and wants the pain of treatment because he believes it necessary to save his life. (2) The person has a rational desire that results in his wanting not to have the rule violated. For example, a defendant desires not to be deprived of freedom, and so he does not want to be convicted and to spend the next year in prison. (3) The person has desires that are relevant to her not wanting a moral rule violated. For example, she does not want to be deprived of freedom, but her desire in this instance is not rational. For example, a young woman desires to be allowed to die because her fiancé has been killed in a motorcycle accident. She does not want doctors to prevent her suicide attempt from succeeding. (4) The person has no desires at all that are relevant to the moral rule violation. For example, a person is so demented that he does not have any desires that would be affected by the proposed violation of the moral rule.

The relevant rational desires of a person are morally relevant even if, because of the lack of relevant rational beliefs, he does not see the connection between his rational desires and the moral rule violation. For example, a patient who has a rational desire to prolong his life even if this means enduring significant pain may refuse a painful operation because he does not realize that it is necessary to prolong his life. Another patient has a rational desire to die rather than to endure continuing significant pain and so refuses a painful operation even though he knows that it is necessary to prolong his life. At least some, if not all, impartial rational persons would publicly allow treating these two patients differently even though both refuse to have the operations.

(b) WHAT ARE THE BELIEFS OF THE PERSON TOWARD WHOM THE RULE IS BEING VIOLATED? Again there are several possibilities. (1) All of a person's beliefs about how she will be affected by the violation are rational and based on adequate evidence. (2) Some of her beliefs about how she will be affected by the violation are rational and based on adequate evidence, but others are either irrational or would be irrational if the person had a higher level of intelligence or knowledge. (3) She has no beliefs about how she will be affected by the violation, or all of her beliefs are irrational or would count as irrational if she had a higher level of intelligence or knowledge.

As shown by the contrast between the two patients who refuse life-prolonging operations, what a person knows about the consequences of her decision may influence whether people would allow violating a moral rule with regard to her. The relevant beliefs of a person, including whether those beliefs are irrational or would be if the person had a higher level of knowledge or intelligence, may determine whether a person is competent to make a rational decision. The rationality or irrationality of a patient's desires may also determine whether a person is competent. Physicians appropriately use whether a patient is competent to make a rational decision when they decide whether to violate a moral rule with regard to a patient for his own benefit, but without his consent, that is, whether to act paternalistically.

Features 3a and 3b are relevant not only in determining competence but also in determining other aspects of valid consent. Consent counts as valid only if the patient has the rational desires and beliefs appropriately related to making his decision. It is generally acknowledged that whether a patient has given valid consent to a medical procedure is morally relevant in determining whether the physician should perform that procedure. As with the other morally relevant features, this feature is morally relevant to a decision only insofar as the agent knows, or should know, that the feature is present, that is, knows, or should know, that the person has the appropriate rational beliefs and desires. That is why actual consent is required in most medical situations. Obtaining a patient's valid consent confirms a physician's belief that the patient has the rational beliefs and desires appropriately related to making his decision.[23]

4. Is the relationship between the person violating the
rule and the persons toward whom the rule is being
violated such that the former sometimes has a duty
to violate moral rules with regard to the latter
independently of their consent?

This feature accounts for the fact that the relationship parents have with their children is morally relevant. When considering the violation of a moral rule, it is morally relevant whether it is the parents of the children who are violating the rule with regard to them. Parents' violations of the rule against depriving of freedom with regard to their children (e.g., making them do their homework) do not count as the same kind of violation as violations of the same rule by adults toward children with regard to whom they have no special duty. This is true even when the evils caused, avoided, and prevented, and the relevant desires and beliefs of the children, are the same.

This feature also explains why the relationship between governments and their citizens is morally relevant. When a government deprives one or more of its citizens of some freedom, that is not the same kind of act as when one citizen deprives another one of the same amount of freedom, even when the evils caused, avoided, and prevented, and the rational desires and beliefs of the person being deprived of the freedom, are the same. Of course, both acts of deprivation might be morally unjustified, but because they are not the same kind of act, one of them might be justified and the other not. For example, a government might be justified in forcing a person to sell his property in order to build a road, whereas no private citizen would be justified in doing so. This feature makes it possible that appropriate members of the government may be justified in inflicting harm on a citizen when people without this special relationship are not justified in inflicting that harm in what may otherwise count as the same kind of situation. This is an essential feature in distinguishing punishment from revenge.

5. Which goods or benefits (including kind, degree, probability, duration, and distribution) are being promoted by the violation?

Except for unrealistic philosophical examples, unless the violation of a moral rule is trivial, this feature is morally relevant only when the previous feature applies or when one has or justifiably expects the immediate consent of the person toward whom the rule is being violated. When the person violating the rule is someone who has a duty to violate moral rules with regard to the person toward whom the rule is being violated, this counts as a political situation. When dealing with individuals who are not in a political situation, Negative Utilitarianism, which counts only harmful consequences as morally relevant, fits our moral judgments far better than Classical Utilitarianism, which treats goods and harms as equally relevant. However, when dealing with governments, the reverse seems to be true. The major Classical Utilitarians, certainly Bentham and probably Mill, were primarily concerned with the actions of governments.

The failure to appreciate, or perhaps even to notice, the significance of the relationship between morally relevant features 4 and 5 may be a factor in explaining why many contemporary philosophers converted a plausible moral system applied to governments into an implausible system applied to individuals. Any theory that counts only the consequences of the particular act as morally relevant results in many counterintuitive moral judgments. However, recognition of the relationship between features 4 and 5 explains the strong points of both Negative and Classical Utilitarianism. It should be explicitly noted that this feature concerns only the promotion of goods; deprivation of goods is the same as causing harms and so is included in feature 2.

*6. Is the rule being violated toward a person
in order to prevent her from violating a moral rule
when her violation would be (a) unjustified
or (b) weakly justified?*

This feature distinguishes between deception by those involved in some kinds of undercover police work and deception by those seeking to gain additional anthropological or sociological knowledge, even when the other morally relevant features are the same. Undercover police who pretend to be gang members in order to prevent criminal activity might be justified in deceiving members of the gang, whereas sociologists who pretend to be gang members of the same gang might not be justified if they are deceiving the gang members in order to gain information for a scholarly article or a book on gangs. Whether an action is an attempt to prevent an unjustified or weakly justified violation of a moral rule can also be used to distinguish between justified and unjustified spying (and other activities) by one government with regard to another. Deception and other violations of the moral rules that are unjustified when employed by a nation planning to attack another may be justified when employed by a nation responding to this planned aggression. Of course, a positive answer to this question does not justify all violations of moral rules; not just anything can be done to prevent violations of moral rules.

Although law enforcement is often thought of as involving the punishment of violations of the law, it also involves prevention of such violations. It may be morally allowed for police to deprive people of freedom by not allowing some public protest when this involves an unjustified or weakly justified violation of the law when it would not be morally allowed for them to deprive people of that same freedom if no law were going to be violated. However, it is plausible that more serious violations of a moral rule might be justified in order to prevent completely unjustified violations (e.g., violations of the law in order to promote segregation) than to prevent weakly justified violations (e.g., violations of the law in order to protest segregation). There is a problem with evaluating this plausible claim because it is extremely difficult to envision that preventing a completely unjustified violation and preventing a weakly justified violation will not also differ in other morally relevant features.

7. Is the rule being violated toward a person because he has violated a moral rule (a) unjustifiably or (b) with a weak justification?

These are crucial features when discussing punishment. It would be inappropriate to call the infliction of harm "punishment" unless the person inflicting the harm has a duty to do so, which is why feature 4, concerning the relationship between the violator of the rule and the person toward whom the rule is violated, is an essential feature when justifying punishment.

This feature, together with feature 4, explains why the infliction of harm that is justifiable as a punishment may not be justifiable when that infliction of harm is not a punishment but all of the other morally relevant features are the same. This feature is also relevant when considering the justified infliction of harm that may not be appropriately called "punishment," for example, harms that are inflicted on a country participating in aggression as responses to their immoral acts. However, this kind of "punishment," like standard punishments, must have prevention of future violations as its justification or it is simply an unjustified act of revenge.

Hobbes was completely clear and correct about this point.[24] It also seems morally relevant whether the violation is weakly justified or completely unjustified.

8. Are there any alternative actions or policies that would be morally preferable?

This feature is often simply included as part of features 2 and 5, which are concerned with the harms and benefits that are caused, avoided, and prevented. But it is not merely the consequences of alternative policies that are morally relevant. An alternative action or policy may be morally preferable to the action being considered because it does not violate a moral rule. Paternalistic deception, which might be justified if there were no nonpaternalistic alternatives, is not justified if there is a preferable alternative, such as taking time to persuade citizens or patients rather than deceiving them. Explicit awareness of this feature may lead people to try to find out if there are any alternative actions that either would not involve a violation of a moral rule or would involve causing much less harm.

The inadequacy of most of the discussions of legalizing physician-assisted suicide is an example of the failure to consider this morally relevant feature. It is admitted by proponents of legalizing physician-assisted suicide that doing so has some risks, such as increasing pressure on terminally ill patients to die sooner and various other kinds of abuse. However, they claim that these risks are significantly outweighed by the benefits of legalizing physician-assisted suicide, such as the elimination of months or years of terrible pain and suffering. If there were no alternative method of eliminating these months or years of terrible pain and suffering, then they would have a strong argument. However, patients are already allowed to refuse food and fluids as well as any medical treatment, so legalizing physician-assisted suicide is not necessary to prevent significant pain and suffering. If patients are educated about this alternative, which, contrary to popular opinion, usually causes no pain, and can always be made completely painless, they can arrange to die as quickly or more quickly than with physician-assisted suicide. The presence of this alternative changes the force of the argument.[25]

9. Is the violation being done intentionally or only knowingly?

Morally relevant features are related only to justifications, not to excuses. A morally relevant feature must be relevant to a decision about whether to commit some violation. If a feature is relevant only to whether a moral judgment should be made or to a moral judgment about the person, that is, whether the feature involves a complete or partial excuse, I consider it to be relevant to judgments of responsibility, not to moral judgments. That is why answers to the following questions are not listed as morally relevant features. Is the violation being done (a) voluntarily or because of a volitional disability, (b) freely or because of coercion, or (c) knowingly or without knowledge of what is being done? (d) Is the lack of knowledge excusable or the result of negligence?[26] Different answers to any of these questions may change the moral judgments made about persons, but only because different answers may provide partial or complete excuses.

The answers to questions (a), (b), (c), and (d) cannot be used to justify a decision or help one to decide whether to commit a violation that has one of these features rather than another. For example, a person cannot decide whether to do an action freely rather than because of coercion. Hence, these features are not useful in deciding whether to violate a moral rule. However, the answer to question 9 might sometimes be useful in deciding whether to violate a moral rule.

Although a person cannot usually decide whether to commit a violation intentionally or only knowingly, sometimes that is possible. For example, a nurse may be willing to administer morphine to terminally ill patients in order to relieve pain even though she knows it will hasten their death, but with no other morally relevant changes in the situation, she would not administer morphine in order to hasten the death of the patient. Many people would agree with the nurse's decision and allow the administration of morphine in the first situation but not the second. This feature explains what is correct in the Doctrine of Double Effect, which states that in some cases where all of the other morally relevant features are the same, it may be morally acceptable to do an act knowingly that it is not morally acceptable to do intentionally.[27]

Usually this doctrine is used when one has to choose between harming two different individuals. Some claim that it is not morally permissible to intentionally cause harm to one person in order to prevent harm to another person. They claim, however, that it is morally permissible to prevent harm to a person if you only know, but do not intend, that your action will result in harm to another. A common example is intentionally killing the fetus to save the life of the mother versus a surgical procedure to save the life of the mother although the surgeon knows it will result in the death of the fetus. The distinction between an action being done intentionally or only knowingly may also account for what many regard as a morally significant difference between lying and other forms of deception, especially withholding information. Lying is always intentionally deceiving, whereas withholding information may often be only knowingly deceiving. Nonetheless, it is important to remember that almost all violations that are morally unacceptable when done intentionally are also morally unacceptable when done only knowingly.

*10. Is the situation an emergency such that people are
not likely to plan to be in that kind of situation?*

This kind of emergency situation is sufficiently rare that, except for
those charged with handling emergencies, people do not expect to
be involved in it, and so the thought of being in it does not affect
their lives. This feature is necessary to account for the fact that
certain kinds of emergency situations change the decisions and
judgments that some would make even when all of the other morally relevant features are the same. For example, in an emergency
when large numbers of people have been seriously injured, doctors
are morally allowed to abandon patients who have a very small
chance of survival in order to take care of those with a better
chance. However, in the ordinary practice of medicine, doctors are
not morally allowed to abandon patients with poor prognoses in
order to treat those with better prognoses, even if doing so will
result in more people surviving. Public knowledge that this procedure is allowed in emergencies will not affect any person's behavior nor should it cause anyone increased anxiety, whereas public
knowledge that this procedure is allowed in the normal practice of
medicine may have profound effects on people's behavior and
anxiety levels.

Failure to realize that whether a situation is an emergency situation is a morally relevant feature explains why philosophers who
hold that only consequences are relevant often use emergency situations as examples in order to show that consequences are the
overriding, if not the sole, morally relevant consideration. They do
not recognize that what is morally acceptable in an emergency situation may not be morally acceptable in nonemergency or normal
situations. Common morality allows breaking a moral rule in an
emergency situation that it would not allow in a nonemergency
situation even when all the other morally relevant features are the

same, including the foreseeable consequences of the particular act. In emergency situations, in order to benefit their patients, physicians are sometimes allowed to deprive them of their freedom and even to inflict pain on them without their consent, when they are not allowed to do so in nonemergency situations that are the same in all of their other morally relevant features.

Summary of morally relevant features

The above list of ten questions generates far more than ten morally relevant features. There is no way to estimate how many such features there might be, for there is no precise way of determining what counts as a single feature. The point of the list is to help guide the search for morally relevant facts. Everyone admits that the correct solution to most moral problems depends on discovering all of the relevant facts, but previously there was no explicit guide to help one determine which facts were morally relevant. But this list of questions is not primarily a checklist to explicitly go through when considering any violation of a moral rule. Those facts that provide answers to any question on the list of ten questions are essential in providing a correct moral description of the act. However, it will often be obvious that some features are not relevant; for example, punishment is never an issue in making moral decisions in medicine.

It has not been shown that the answers to the preceding questions are the only morally relevant features. However, like the moral rules, a feature does not count as morally relevant unless it can be formulated in a way that is understandable to all moral agents. Only features that can be formulated so as to be understandable to all moral agents can be part of common morality. This is not merely a theoretical requirement; as a practical matter, requiring this level of generality is needed to ensure the kind of impartiality required by morality. Without this level of generality it would be possible to manipulate descriptions of violations in a way that would allow a person to benefit his friends or colleagues. For example, a doctor might allow doctors to deceive patients in situations that are morally identical to those in which she would not allow nondoctors to deceive.

Requiring the morally relevant features to be stated in terms that are understandable by all moral agents may make them seem too abstract and general. It may be valuable to describe the morally relevant features in a less general way and to provide particular examples of morally relevant features. Although all of these more detailed descriptions of features must be instances of the more general features in the list, providing examples and describing the features in more detail may give them more force. For purposes of describing the moral system, however, the completely general characterization of the morally relevant features represented by the answers to the above list of questions is sufficient.

The second step: Estimating the consequences of everyone knowing that a kind of violation is allowed and that it is not allowed

Describing a violation using only those facts that are morally relevant, that is, those facts that are answers to one of the ten questions listed in the previous section, determines what counts as the same kind of violation. Then the consequences of everyone knowing that this kind of violation is allowed must be estimated, and also the consequences of everyone knowing that this kind of violation is not allowed. The term "estimated" is used rather than some word like "determined" in order to make clear that the procedure for determining the consequences of everyone knowing that this kind of violation is allowed and of everyone knowing that this kind of violation is not allowed does not usually yield precise results. This is especially true of particular violations by individuals. When considering violations by governments—for example, when estimating the consequences of alternative tax laws (which deprive citizens of some of their money)—there may be sufficient empirical research to make more accurate estimates. However, even when considering government policies, there is usually a range of acceptable estimates, some of which would favor one policy and some of which would favor another. But sometimes, even in particular violations by individuals, these estimates are clear enough to arrive at an answer to a case about which people initially disagree.

Considering the consequences of deception being publicly allowed to obtain consent for a needed operation alerts one to the far greater harm that is risked by deception, even in the particular case, that is, a general loss of trust, especially in medical situations. If a patient discovers he has been deceived and tells other patients, it is extremely likely that all of these patients will have less trust in what they are told. Although there might be a very small chance of any of this happening, if it does happen the consequences could be serious.[28] The chances of any particular house being burned down are very small, yet in normal situations most people regard it as imprudent not to buy fire insurance. Cheating often has no bad results in the particular case, but publicly allowing cheating, except in extraordinary circumstances, would almost always have far worse consequences than if it was not publicly allowed. Unjustified violations of the first five moral rules almost always cause more harm than they prevent in the particular case, but this is not true for unjustified violations of the second five moral rules. The need for the second step of the two-step procedure is shown more clearly by considering violations of the second five moral rules than by considering violations of the first five. Without this second step many acts of deceiving, breaking promises, cheating, breaking a law, or neglecting a duty, which everyone recognizes to be immoral, would not be correctly accounted for.[29]

::
Moral Virtues and Vices

People do not explicitly use the moral system when making their moral decisions and judgments. People also do not explicitly use a grammatical system when speaking and when interpreting the speech of others. Children learn to make the right moral decisions and judgments in the same way that they learn to speak correctly. They listen and watch adults making moral decisions and judgments, and they are praised when they make correct decisions and judgments and are corrected when they make mistaken decisions and judgments. If they are provided with good examples and good teaching, and they are not unlucky, they may come to develop moral virtues. Children acquire moral virtues by observing, learning, and performing the appropriate behavior when confronted with moral situations for a long enough time. If they develop these virtues, they can respond appropriately in moral situations without having to stop and think about how to act.

It is significant that there is no moral virtue related to following any of the first five moral rules. No one is expected to unjustifiably violate any of these rules and so is not regarded as having any praiseworthy trait of character for not doing so. However, cruelty is a moral vice that, although primarily related to the intentional unjustified breaking of the rule prohibiting the causing of pain, can be related to the intentional unjustified breaking of any of the first five rules. The virtue that may seem to correspond to cruelty is kindness, but kindness is not related to the moral rules at all, but rather to justified following of the moral ideals. The vice that corresponds to kindness is callousness. Callousness is a moral vice that involves failing to act on moral ideals in circumstances where rational persons would expect most people to so act. None of the first five rules has a specific moral virtue associated with it, although cruelty is a vice commonly associated with violating the rule prohibiting causing pain.

Moral virtues and moral vices can be associated with each of the second five moral rules. Truthfulness can be related to the rule "Do not deceive," dependability to "Keep your promises," fairness to "Do not cheat," honesty to "Obey the law," and conscientiousness to "Do your duty." The corresponding vices that can be associated with these rules are deceitfulness, undependability, unfairness, dishonesty, and neglectfulness. This particular pairing of the moral virtues and vices and the second five moral rules is somewhat arbitrary. Our moral language is not quite so precise. But all of the recognized moral virtues and vices are related to either the moral rules or the moral ideals. They all involve using the moral system as a guide for one's behavior or failing to use it as such a guide.

Having a moral virtue does not entail never violating the associated moral rule. A truthful person does not always tell the truth. When deception is strongly justified, a truthful person deceives. Someone who always tells the truth is tactless, not truthful. A truthful person does not unjustifiably violate the rule prohibiting deception. The same is true for all of the other moral virtues. They all require knowing (but do not require being able to articulate) when it is justified to break the moral rule. There are no precise rules for attributing these virtues and vices to a person. Making moral judgments about people, rather than actions, is related to an appraisal of how much the person exceeds or falls below what rational persons would expect of people.

In addition to the moral virtues and vices, there are also personal virtues and vices. Courage, prudence, and temperance are personal virtues; cowardice, imprudence, and intemperance are personal

vices. Unlike the moral virtues, the personal virtues are not necessarily related to acting morally. These personal virtues are essential for having the moral virtues, but as both Hobbes and Kant
point out, having all of these personal virtues is compatible not only
with having no moral virtues but also with having many moral
vices. All of the personal virtues, not just the three mentioned above
but also such traits as fortitude and patience, can make an immoral
person even more dangerous. Although the personal virtues are
those virtues everyone wants to have personally, having them does
not rule out acting immorally.

The traits of character that most resemble the moral virtues and
vices are the social virtues and vices. These virtues, such as friendliness and gratitude or being appreciative, are traits of character that
lead to social harmony. Disharmony may increase the suffering of
harms, so these virtues are normally not distinguished from the
moral virtues, nor is there normally any need to do so. However,
these virtues are not directly related to the moral rules and ideals,
and the corresponding social vices should not be regarded as moral
vices. We may not like people who are unfriendly and not appreciative, but unlike most of the moral vices, these social vices do not
necessarily involve the violation of any moral rule. Even though
most of these virtues can be thought of as involving following the
moral ideals, and the social vices as failing to follow these ideals,
they seem more closely related to the utilitarian ideals. Most important, exemplifying them never justifies violating a moral rule, as
is the case with all of the moral virtues, properly so called.

Summary and Test

Although much more needs to be said to provide a full description
of common morality, all of its essential elements have been

identified. The moral system, which includes the moral rules, the moral ideals, and the two-step procedure for justifying violations of the moral rules, including the morally relevant features, has been described. This description of the moral system is sufficient so that each reader can test its adequacy in the following way.

Consider a situation that calls for you to make a moral decision because a moral rule, on your interpretation of it, applies to this situation. Then consider whether the situation involves violating the moral rule with regard to a moral agent or some being who is not a moral agent. If the latter, consider whether, with respect to following that moral rule, the being belongs to the group that you hold is impartially protected by morality. If not, consider how much, if at all, you hold that morality protects that kind of being. Then, identify all of the morally relevant features of the violation and describe the act using only those features. Next, estimate the consequences of everyone knowing that this kind of violation is allowed and of everyone knowing that this kind of violation is not allowed. Finally, rank the harmful and beneficial consequences of these two estimates. If all of these steps are adequately performed, the test of this description of morality is whether you agree, at least after reflection, with the moral decision or judgment that you arrived at by this explicit use of the moral system. (Using the flow chart concerning morality on page 152 may be helpful in applying the test.)

Part II :: The Moral Theory

In the first part of this book, I described the moral system that is common morality. That description may have made it seem obvious that all moral agents would endorse adopting this moral system, but that is not true. Not all rational persons would favor requiring everyone to act morally with regard to at least all other moral agents. If they belong to a dominant group, rational persons might not even pretend to favor all moral agents acting morally toward all moral agents.[1] All rational persons do want everyone to obey the moral rules with regard to themselves and those for whom they are concerned.[2] They also want everyone to follow the moral ideals with regard to themselves and those for whom they are concerned. They probably even want everyone to follow utilitarian ideals, for example, promoting pleasure, with regard to themselves and their friends. But to want everyone to act morally with regard to oneself and those for whom one cares is not the same as endorsing morality—in particular, it is not endorsing the adoption of a moral system that prohibits immoral behavior toward any moral agent.

::
The Justification of Morality

Showing that all moral agents would endorse adopting a moral system that required everyone to act morally with regard to, at least, all other moral agents is what I regard as providing a justification of morality. But unless certain conditions are satisfied, it is not possible to show that all rational persons would endorse morality. One of the conditions required for the justification of morality is that rational persons use only those beliefs that are shared by all rational persons. To say that such a rational person endorses morality means that he holds, at least publicly, that immoral behavior should be prohibited and morally good behavior encouraged and that everyone should be taught to act morally. However, almost everyone already does, at least publicly, endorse morality. Philosophical theories often consist of arguments for what everyone already knows. These arguments are presented, not so much to persuade, but to clarify the views that everyone already holds. My arguments showing under what conditions and why all rational persons favor teaching people to act morally, prohibiting immoral behavior, and encouraging people to do morally good actions are intended in this way.

Each moral agent knows that all moral agents want her to obey the moral rules with regard to themselves; indeed, she knows that all moral agents want everyone to obey the moral rules with regard to themselves. This may explain the appeal of Kant's claim that the demands of morality are categorical, not hypothetical; that is, they do not depend on the goals that a person has. Every rational person is aware that all people want her, regardless of any ends she might have, not to act immorally, at least with regard to themselves. It is also extremely plausible to hold that she is aware that she wants everyone else to act morally, at least with regard to herself. This may explain the appeal of Kant's claim that all rational persons realize that they themselves put forward the moral system that governs their own behavior as well as the behavior of everyone else. It should not be surprising that great philosophers such as Kant have significant insights even when their theories are fundamentally misguided.

However, some rational people might not support common morality. Rational persons might hold some religious beliefs that allow, encourage, or even require that they violate the moral rules with regard to those with different religious beliefs. Some people who belong to a dominant group might support moral behavior only with regard to other members of this group but not with regard to those in any subordinate group. This dominant group can be a racial group, an ethnic group, a religious group, or even a whole nation or state. Of course, they do not expect those in the subordinate groups to willingly act morally toward them, but they might be unconcerned about this, for they might believe, perhaps correctly, that they have sufficient power to protect themselves. If rational persons have any of these kinds of beliefs, they need not even claim to endorse common morality.

Only if they do not make use of any beliefs that are not shared by all rational persons, which I call "putting on the blindfold of justice," is it irrational for people not to endorse morality. Only when the beliefs they use are limited to those beliefs that all rational persons hold, what I call rationally required beliefs, must all rational persons endorse morality. This limitation on the beliefs that can be used means that rational agents cannot use their religious or scientific beliefs or their knowledge of their special status as reasons for not endorsing common morality.[3] It also means that if a person is putting forward an attitude toward morality to be accepted by the persons she is talking to, she can use only the knowledge that they also have all of the features of moral agents, including the rationally required beliefs and desires.[4] Under this limitation and in this circumstance she must put forward the moral attitude toward the moral rules; that is, she must endorse common morality as a public system to be applied to all moral agents. This restriction on the beliefs that can be used also makes it irrational for her to refuse to endorse morality when others put it forward. To refuse to endorse morality makes it more likely that the people she is talking to will regard her as a dangerous person. Because she has no reason to refuse and refusing increases her chances of suffering harm, to do so would be acting irrationally.

Rational persons want to avoid death, pain, disability, loss of freedom, and loss of pleasure, and they know not only that they are fallible and vulnerable but that they can be deceived and harmed by other people. They know that if people do not act morally with regard to them, they will be at significantly increased risk of suffering some harm. If they use only rationally required beliefs, it would be irrational not to endorse common morality as the system to be adopted to govern the behavior of all moral agents, unless they had some reason for not endorsing it. Given the restrictions to rationally required beliefs, they can have no such reason. Under these conditions, all rational persons will at least claim to hold that everyone, themselves included, should obey the moral rules with regard to all others, that everyone should be taught to act morally, that immoral behavior should be prohibited, and that morally good behavior should be encouraged.

However, it must be kept in mind that in endorsing common morality, a rational person is not endorsing a system that provides a unique answer to every moral question. Rational persons, even with the limitation to rationally required beliefs, know that if they want agreement with all moral agents, which is the other condition required for the justification of morality, the system they put forward must allow for some differences.[5] Within limits, common morality allows for rational persons to disagree about (1) the scope of morality, (2) the rankings of the harms and benefits, (3) views about human nature, and (4) interpretations of the moral rules. In endorsing common morality, rational persons are adopting only a framework to govern their moral decisions and judgments; they are allowing themselves some latitude in deciding controversial issues. They realize they will need some way to settle the controversial issues not settled by common morality. This is why all of the great moral philosophers, Aristotle, Hobbes, Kant, and Mill, supplement their account of morality with a political theory.

Rational persons who use only rationally required beliefs and seek agreement with other moral agents about whom they know only that they are moral agents with all of the rationally required beliefs and desires must endorse morality. This is the strongest justification of morality that it is possible to provide.[6] Rational persons who use beliefs that are not shared by all need not care about reaching agreement with all other moral agents, and so need not endorse morality. They can regard religion, race, or country as more important than morality. It is not irrational of them to do this. But if they do this, they are using beliefs other than those shared by all rational persons. Only by limiting persons to using only rationally required beliefs is it possible to show that all rational persons would endorse morality to all other moral agents, that is, to justify morality. If a person uses some specialized belief, even if it is not irrational, she need not endorse the same system to govern the behavior of everyone as those rational persons who use only rationally required beliefs. A rational person who uses beliefs about his own special status need not endorse common morality because it requires obeying the moral rules impartially with regard to all moral agents, and such a guide may severely limit his own freedom with no benefit to anyone for whom he is concerned.

Unless they use some specialized knowledge, all rational persons seeking agreement with other moral agents about whom they know only that they also have the rationally required beliefs and desires would claim to support morality. This explains why politicians, when they are talking to an audience about whom they know only that it consists of moral agents, always support morality. It is only when a politician knows that all of his audience belongs to some ethnic, national, racial, or religious group that he might not offer unconditional support of common morality. When talking to an individual or a group about whom she knows only that they also have the rationally required beliefs and desires, every rational person who uses only rationally required beliefs endorses morality. But this does not mean that she actually intends to act morally. As La Rochefoucauld pointed out, "Hypocrisy is the homage that vice pays to virtue." Hypocrisy, far from showing that morality is a sham, shows how powerful it is. For most people in normal circumstances, it would be irrational to tell others that you do not support morality. Only those who know that the group to whom they are talking shares their nationalistic, racial, or religious views, or those who believe that they belong to a group that has sufficient power to ignore the interests of others, can rationally refuse to endorse common morality.

This justification of common morality is far more conditional than many philosophers have wanted. Although many social-contract theorists agree that all rational agents will endorse morality only if the beliefs they use are limited in some way, Kant seems to hold that, even without any limitation on beliefs, all rational agents would still endorse morality. Many philosophers admit that all rational persons will endorse morality only if they are seeking agreement with all rational persons; however, Kant puts forward an account of rationality that he claims results in all rational persons endorsing morality independently of their seeking to reach such agreement. Kant even holds that it is irrational to act immorally. However, if rationality and irrationality are taken as the fundamental normative concepts, that is, if all moral agents agree that no one should ever act irrationally, it is not irrational to act immorally. Attempts to provide an unconditional justification of morality or to show that it is irrational to act immorally result in rationality and irrationality no longer being fundamental normative concepts.

It becomes possible for a person whom everyone would consider to be a moral agent to intelligibly ask, "Why should I act rationally?"

Characteristics of Moral Agents

I have admitted that morality can be justified only conditionally. The primary condition is that people use only those beliefs that all moral agents have. Morality must be known to all moral agents to ensure that it cannot require beliefs that some of them do not have. Thus, this condition is not arbitrary. When I talk about the beliefs that all moral agents share, I mean those beliefs that any person must have in order to be a moral agent. There may be other beliefs that all rational persons share, but they are irrelevant to the justification of morality. Before I discuss the content of the beliefs that all moral agents share, I shall discuss some other features that a person must have in order to be a moral agent, that is, to be subject to moral judgment.

To be a moral agent, a person must have at least a certain minimal intelligence, including some ability to reason. This minimal intelligence involves being able to make at least the kinds of simple inferences that we expect children age ten and older to make. For example, they must be able to infer that this person wants to avoid pain from the fact that all rational persons want to avoid pain and that this person is rational. It also involves the ability to use past experience as a guide. A moral agent must be able to know at least the immediate and short-term consequences of most of her actions. Moral agents need not be sophisticated in their use of deductive and inductive reasoning, but unless they have conflicting evidence, they must not only accept simple deductive and inductive inferences but make them spontaneously when such inferences are relevant to their decisions. Also, unless they have conflicting evidence, they must believe that the world is as they perceive it to be.

A moral agent must also not have any relevant volitional disabilities.[7] She must be able to believe whatever the overwhelming evidence supports. She must also be able to act on her beliefs. She must be able to act rationally, which requires almost always acting rationally, for there can be no adequate reasons for acting irrationally. Insofar as a person lacks the relevant minimal intelligence or has relevant volitional disabilities, she is not a moral agent and is excused from moral judgment. Actions that are unjustified violations of moral rules do not count as immoral actions if the person is completely excused. To claim to have a complete excuse is to claim to be exempt from moral judgment. To claim to have less than a complete excuse is to claim to be liable to less punishment than someone with no excuse at all.

::
Knowledge or Beliefs Required
of All Moral Agents

Among the facts that all moral agents must believe or know are some facts about human beings. These facts include the following: people not only are mortal but can be killed by other people; people not only suffer pain but can be caused to suffer pain by other people; people not only can become disabled but can be disabled by other people; people not only can lose their freedom but can be deprived of freedom by other people; and people not only can suffer a loss of pleasure but can be deprived of pleasure by others. These facts can be summarized by saying that people are not only vulnerable but can be harmed by other people. All moral agents also know that no one knows everything, and not only do all people make mistakes but other people can deceive them. People have limited knowledge and are fallible. Each moral agent also knows that she herself, like all other persons, is vulnerable, has limited knowledge, is fallible, and can be harmed and deceived by other people.

In addition to these facts about human beings, moral agents know something about the desires of rational persons. They know that unless a rational person has an adequate reason for wanting to die or to suffer pain, disability, or a loss of freedom or pleasure, she does not want these things to happen to her. Because she knows that other people can cause these things to happen to her, she does not want anyone to kill her, cause her pain or disability, or deprive her of freedom or pleasure, unless she has some reason. All moral agents know these facts about themselves and about all other moral agents. Insofar as a person doubts any of these facts, that counts against her being a moral agent, that is, as fully responsible for her actions. Although no one doubts that all moral agents, unless they have a reason, desire to avoid the harms listed above, everyone is aware that, within limits, moral agents rank these harms differently. Also no one doubts that no moral agent, unless she has a reason, wants to avoid consciousness, ability, freedom, or pleasure, but everyone is aware that, within limits, moral agents rank these goods differently.

No one doubts any of the facts about individual moral agents cited in the previous paragraphs. Nor is there any doubt about the following social facts. Although individual acts of deceiving, promise-breaking, cheating, law-breaking, and neglect of duties need not result in anyone suffering any harm, widespread deception, promise-breaking, cheating, law-breaking, and neglect of duties make it significantly more likely that people will lose goods and suffer harms. Knowledge of widespread deception, promise-breaking, cheating, law-breaking, and neglect of duties decreases the amount of trust that people have in one another, which decreases people's opportunities to work together to achieve shared goals. It is no accident that the well-being of a country is very highly correlated with the amount of trust that its citizens have in each other.

In addition to these facts about rational persons, moral agents must also know all of those facts about the world that it would be irrational for any moral agent to doubt. Many of these facts are presupposed by the facts about rational persons presented above. These facts—that there is an external world which has existed for a very long time, that there are other people in it, and that we can often know what has happened and what some of the consequences of our actions will be—are sometimes challenged by philosophical skeptics. However, except for philosophical discussion and writing, philosophers who challenge these facts do not behave any differently than philosophers who do not challenge them. Indeed, they do not behave any differently than people who are not philosophers at all. Given that real doubts affect a person's nonphilosophical behavior, philosophical skeptics have no real doubts about the existence of the external world or other people.

All moral agents believe or know all of these facts. None of these beliefs depends on any special knowledge that is not available to all persons living in any society. By limiting themselves to these beliefs, that is, "putting on the blindfold of justice," moral agents can avoid the almost inevitable biases that might influence the moral system that they would advocate or accept. Like the "veil of ignorance" that John Rawls proposes in his classic *A Theory of Justice*,[8] this blindfold of justice guarantees impartiality. But it also does both more and less than the veil of ignorance. It rules out using even well-established scientific beliefs and thereby guarantees that morality does not require beliefs that are not known to all moral agents. However, unlike the veil of ignorance, the blindfold of justice does not require that all moral agents rank all of the harms and benefits in the same way. Thus, it guarantees impartiality without requiring all moral agents to agree in all of their moral judgments.

All moral agents retain their own, perhaps idiosyncratic, ranking of these harms and benefits, as long as that ranking is within the range of rational rankings. It is rational to rank the chronic pains accompanying some maladies as worse than death, and it is also rational to rank death as worse than suffering these pains. It is not rational to rank the loss of a momentary pleasure as worse than death. Different rational people also rank the loss of a specific kind and amount of ability both higher and lower than a pain of a specific intensity and duration. Any ranking of harms and benefits by any sufficiently large group of otherwise rational persons counts as a rational ranking. Otherwise rational persons are those persons who avoid suffering any of the harms themselves unless they have a reason for doing so and unless they regard that reason as adequate.

⠶
Irrationality and Rationality

Throughout my discussion of morality and its justification, I have talked about the actions, beliefs, and desires of rational persons. On my account, moral agents are rational persons with sufficient knowledge and intelligence to know what the moral rules prohibit and require, and who have the ability to guide their behavior by their knowledge. When talking about rational persons, I am talking about persons only insofar as their actions, beliefs, and desires are rational, but I have not yet provided a detailed explicit account of rationality and irrationality. This was not confusing or misleading, because I am using "rational" and "irrational" in such a way that no person who is responsible for his actions would ever ask, "Why should I act rationally?" or "Why shouldn't I act irrationally?" That is, I am using them as the fundamental normative concepts. Although this is not the only ordinary use of "rational" and "irrational," it is not only an ordinary use but probably the most common everyday use of these concepts.

Not only is this concept of rationality essential to the justification of morality, but an adequate account of morality must be such that it is never irrational to act as morality encourages or requires. If it ever were irrational, then all rational persons must recommend that no one for whom they are concerned, including themselves in that situation, act as morality encourages or requires. However, rational persons who are impartial with respect to the moral rules with regard to all moral agents must recommend that everyone for whom they are concerned, including themselves in that situation, act as morality requires. Impartial rational persons are rational persons, so there is a contradiction.[9]

When the concepts of rationality and irrationality are used as the fundamental normative concepts, they are too important for their meaning to remain implicit. As the fundamental normative concepts, it may be as important to provide a clear, coherent, and comprehensive description of them as it is to provide such a description of morality. Within the limits of this section I cannot provide such a description, but I shall try to make explicit all those features of the concepts of rationality and irrationality that I made use of in my discussion of morality and its justification.

My claims about the actions, beliefs, and desires of rational persons are not based on empirical studies of rational persons; rather, they are based on analyses of the concepts of rationality and irrationality. When I say that all rational persons would perform some action, hold some belief, or have some desire, I mean that an analysis of irrationality shows that it is irrational not to perform that action, hold that belief, or have that desire. When I say that no rational person would perform some action, hold some belief, or have some desire, I mean that an analysis of irrationality shows that it is irrational to perform that action, hold that belief, or have that desire. When I say that rational persons disagree, I mean that an analysis of irrationality shows that it is not irrational either to perform that action or not to perform it, to hold some belief or not to hold it, or to have some desire or not to have it. Generally, these claims about agreement and disagreement of all rational persons depend upon their being limited to rationally required beliefs, but it should be clear when this limitation does not apply.

I realize that the terms "rational" and "irrational" are used in a wide variety of ways; however, I am concerned only with the sense of "rational" and "irrational" that applies when they are used as the basic evaluative or normative terms pertaining to actions. In this sense of "rational" and "irrational," it makes no sense to ask, "Why should I act rationally?" or "Why shouldn't I act irrationally?" No moral agent who uses "rational" and "irrational" in the sense with which I am concerned would ever ask these questions. To ask these questions would show either that the person was not using "rational" and "irrational" in the fundamental normative sense, or that he should not be taken as responsible for his actions.

Irrationality is a simpler concept than rationality. Starting with the concept of irrationality makes it far easier to arrive at a concept of rationality such that no moral agent would ever ask, "Why should I act rationally?" No person who is responsible for her actions would ever advocate to any person for whom she is concerned, including herself, that the person act irrationally. Thus, no one can ever be in a situation where all of the available options are irrational. To appraise an action as irrational is to claim that it should not be done. In a situation in which no other people are involved and all the options are harmful to oneself, if they are not equally harmful, then it is rational to choose the least harmful. It may even be rationally required to choose to suffer an evil if all other choices would result in greater evils. If all the options are equally harmful, it is rationally allowed to choose any of them. All moral agents would advocate to every person for whom they are concerned, including themselves, that the person never act irrationally.

If an action is rational, it does not follow that every moral agent would advocate to every person for whom she is concerned, including herself, that she act in that way. Many rational actions are such that it is rational either to do them or not to do them; that is, they are only rationally allowed. It makes no sense to ask, "Why should I act rationally?" because this question means the same as "Why shouldn't I act irrationally?" Not only does it make sense to ask, "Why should I do this particular rational act?" but it can be rational to advise someone, including oneself, not to do it. It does not make sense to ask, "Why shouldn't I do this particular irrational act?" for no one should ever do any irrational act.

This fundamental evaluative or normative sense of "rational" and "irrational" is the sense of these terms in which philosophers are primarily interested or, if they are not, should be. It is only in this sense of "rational" and "irrational" that showing that all rational persons endorse morality counts as justifying morality. If "irrational" and "rational" are used in a sense such that a moral agent can sensibly ask, "Why should I act rationally?" or "Why shouldn't I act irrationally?" then she need not care if all rational persons endorse morality or anything else. Most philosophers are concerned with the fundamental evaluative or normative sense of "rational" and "irrational" with which I am concerned. However, they have not realized the necessity of showing that their analyses of these concepts make it senseless to ask, "Why should I advocate to those for whom I care that they act rationally?" or "Why should I advocate to those for whom I care that they not act irrationally?" The result is that on all of their analyses of rationality and irrationality, a moral agent could advocate to people for whom she is concerned, including herself, that they act irrationally.

⠶

Rationality as Maximizing Satisfaction of Desires

The mistakes involved fall into two broad categories. The first is that "rationality" is defined prior to and independently of defining "irrationality." This is the result of not recognizing that irrationality is more fundamental than rationality.[10] The second is that "rationality" is defined by means of some formula that does not specify any content for an irrational action. A widely accepted definition that exemplifies both of these mistakes is *"acting rationally is acting so as to maximize the overall satisfaction of one's desires."* On this account, any action that is not consistent with maximizing the overall satisfaction of a person's desires is not a rational action. Most people are not usually aware of whether a particular action is consistent with the overall satisfaction of their desires; indeed, they usually do not even know what would count as the overall satisfaction of their desires. In order to avoid the absurd conclusion that most people do not know whether their intentional actions are irrational, the concept of a nonrational action is introduced. Only actions that people know are consistent with the overall satisfaction of their desires are rational; only actions people know are inconsistent with the overall satisfaction of their desires are irrational. But the conclusion that most intentional actions of most persons are nonrational is equally absurd. Even worse, on this account of a rational action a person who, because of a serious mental disorder, maximizes the satisfaction of his desires by harming himself with no compensating benefit for anyone is acting rationally. But no moral agent who is concerned with such a person would ever advocate that he do such an action.

Those who put forward the maximizing satisfaction of desires account of rationality, or any of its variations, simply overlook the fact that some people have mental disorders that do not involve having false beliefs. Some people with serious mental disorders have a set of desires such that maximizing their overall satisfaction would result in their seriously harming themselves without any compensating benefit to anyone, including themselves.[11] No one who is concerned with these people would ever advocate that they perform such actions. On the contrary, all moral agents concerned with such people would advocate that they never perform such actions. Yet, on the view of rational actions as those that maximize the overall satisfaction of the agent's desires, such actions would be classified as rational. Even more absurd, if one of these people has a weak desire to see a psychiatrist in order to get rid of these other, stronger desires, acting on that desire would count as nonrational or irrational because it conflicts with the overall satisfaction of the person's desires.

Many modifications have been offered to the maximization of the overall satisfaction of desires account of rational actions, but none of them succeeds in providing an account of the content of a rational action that does not have clear counterexamples. Even if acting on any false beliefs about what it would be like to satisfy any particular desire is ruled out, a person with a mental disorder might still have a set of desires such that their maximum satisfaction requires him to act so as to cause himself serious harm with no benefit to anyone.[12] No account that provides a positive definition of a rational action rather than a negative definition of a rational action as one that is not irrational is adequate. Nor does any attempt to provide a content for rational or irrational actions simply by means of a formula provide an adequate account of the fundamental evaluative or normative sense of "rational" and "irrational."

##::
Objectively Irrational Actions

In the objective sense of "irrational," no moral agent would ever advocate to any person for whom she is concerned that he act irrationally. The precise definition is: *A person correctly appraises an intentional action as objectively irrational when he correctly believes that (1) it will cause, or significantly increase the probability of, the agent's suffering (avoidable) death, pain, disability, loss of freedom, or loss of pleasure, and (2) there is no objectively adequate reason for the action.* Any intentional action that is not irrational is rational. In order to arrive at a complete specification of the content of an irrational action, an analysis of an objectively adequate reason must be provided.

In the objective sense of "a reason" such that a reason can make some otherwise irrational action rational, a person correctly believes that there is *an objective reason for an action when he correctly believes that the action will avoid, prevent, relieve, or significantly decrease the probability of (avoidable) death, pain, disability, loss of freedom, or loss of pleasure or that it will cause or significantly increase the probability of (greater) consciousness, ability, freedom, or pleasure for anyone.*[13] A person regards an objective reason as adequate if he regards the harms avoided, prevented, or relieved by the action, or the goods that will be promoted by it, as making it rational to suffer the harms the agent will be caused by it. *A reason is objectively adequate if any significant group of otherwise rational persons regard it as adequate.*[14]

On this account, any intentional action of a person is appraised as rational if it is not irrational. This has the desired result that almost all of the intentional actions of almost everyone are appraised as rational actions. Of course, this results in "rational" not serving as a significant term of praise or commendation, but this is as it should be. Calling an action "rational" simply rules out the most universally shared kind of condemnation, namely, that the act is irrational. People need not endorse an action simply because it is rational. It is quite common for people planning a vacation together to put forward different rational alternatives and to argue for one of them and against all of the others. It is a common practice in medicine for a physician, who has a duty to inform the patient of all of the rational alternatives, to argue in favor of one or more of them and to argue against the others. Only if an action is rationally required must everyone favor doing it.

Most rational actions are such that it is rational both to do the action and to not do it. Choosing which movie to go to, what food to order from the menu, which course to take, and so on, are usually rationally allowed actions or choices. The only rationally required actions are those for which the only alternative is irrational. In normal circumstances it is rationally required to get out of the way of a speeding truck. In many acute medical situations it is rationally required to accept the treatment proposed by the physician, such as taking the prescribed antibiotic for a very serious bacterial infection. However, in many other medical situations there is often more than one rational treatment, such as treating a bad back with surgery or by a combination of rest and exercise. In many others it may even be rational to refuse all treatment. It is rationally allowed for a terminally ill cancer patient for whom all life-prolonging treatments involve significant discomfort to refuse all treatments.

Actions that are appraised as objectively irrational may be the result of the agent's lack of information. When the person appraising the action knows something that the agent does not, he may appraise the action as irrational even though it is more in accord with common usage to describe that action as mistaken. An objectively irrational action need not count at all as evidence that the agent has a mental disorder. It may only count as evidence that he is inadequately informed of the consequences of his action. However, some objectively irrational actions are the result, not of inadequate information, but of a mental disorder or of some strong emotion, such as anger or fear. Someone suffering from a mental disorder or some strong emotion may act in a way that he knows, or should know, is objectively irrational. This kind of objectively irrational action is also personally irrational and counts as evidence that the person has a mental disorder.

When an action is appraised as objectively irrational, it is appraised as irrational independently of any consideration about whether it counts as evidence that the person doing the action has a mental disorder. Its irrationality is the result of the facts believed by the person who appraises it as irrational. The beliefs or knowledge, or lack of beliefs or lack of knowledge, of the agent have no special status in determining the objective irrationality of an action. An action a person appraises as objectively irrational is the kind of action that he would never advocate that anyone for whom he is concerned, including himself, ever do. Unless I indicate otherwise, whenever I talk about an irrational action, I mean an action that is appraised as objectively irrational. Such actions have the content that I specified at the beginning of this section: they are believed to result in the agent suffering some harm, or being at a significantly increased risk of suffering some harm, and to have no objectively adequate reason to be done.

Personally Irrational Actions

When the person appraising an action as objectively irrational is the agent himself, and he still acts in the way that he has appraised as irrational, his action is also personally irrational. Such actions count as evidence that the person has a mental disorder. Even if the agent does not appraise the action as irrational, but he should know the facts that make it objectively irrational, then that action is also personally irrational. When an act that is objectively irrational is also an act that is personally irrational, this is due to a mental disorder or to an overpowering desire or emotion. However, when the person who appraises an act as irrational is not the agent, many actions that are appraised as objectively irrational are not personally irrational. In these cases, the agent does not have the information that would or should lead him to appraise his action as irrational. In unusual circumstances, an act that is appraised as personally irrational may not be appraised as objectively irrational. The appraiser and the agent can both have information that the agent will be harmed by the action, but the appraiser might know that there is an adequate reason for the self-harming action while the agent believes that there is no adequate reason, or if she does believe that there is, this belief does not motivate her.

A person correctly appraises an action as personally irrational when he correctly believes (1) that the agent knows or expects, or should know or expect, that her action will cause her to suffer any of the harms or significantly increase the probability that she will suffer any of them, and (2) the agent believes that there is no objectively adequate reason for the action, or if she does believe there is an objectively adequate reason, this belief does not motivate her.[15] An agent should know or expect that her action will cause or significantly increase the probability of her suffering any of the harms when, in this situation, almost everyone else with similar knowledge and intelligence would know or expect this. A person has a reason in a personal sense when she has a rational belief about the world such that if her belief is true, there is a fact that is an objective reason for doing the action. She has a personally adequate reason when she has a rational belief about the world such that if her belief is true, there is a fact that is an objectively adequate reason for doing the action. A person has a reason in a personal sense even if her belief does not motivate her to act. But having such a nonmotivating reason does not make an action that would otherwise be a personally irrational action a personally rational one.

As pointed out above, many objectively irrational actions are due to lack of information by the agent and do not count as evidence that the agent has a mental disorder. Actions that are personally irrational are also usually objectively irrational. If a person, due to a mental disorder or some overpowering desire or emotion, acts in a way that he knows will cause him harm and he has no beliefs that there will be compensating benefits for anyone, then that action will normally also be objectively irrational. However, although it would be unusual, a person might advocate to someone for whom he cares that he act in a personally irrational way because he has additional information and so does not appraise the action as objectively irrational. For example, a person may want to have his arm cut off simply because he wants to be asymmetrical, which is irrational. But his friend may recommend that he have his arm amputated because he knows that the person has a cancer in his arm that will kill him if he does not have it amputated.

Many actions that are objectively irrational are not personally irrational. The fact that there are examples of actions that are personally irrational but not objectively irrational shows that an action that is irrational in either sense need not be irrational in the other. A person who plans to commit suicide by volunteering for what he believes to be a dangerous but worthwhile medical experiment, solely in order to make his wife and children feel guilty, is planning to act in a personally irrational way. If he is not motivated at all by his belief that the experiment will benefit others, but only by his desire to die and make his family feel guilty, he is acting irrationally in the personal sense. However, a friend who knows that the experiment is not all that dangerous and who recognizes that the benefits to others provide an adequate reason for volunteering may advocate that the person volunteer for the experiment, even though it is a personally irrational action. It is only objectively irrational actions that no one would ever advocate to anyone for whom he is concerned. However, personally irrational actions count as evidence that the person has a mental disorder, even if the action is not objectively irrational.

In these accounts of both objectively irrational actions and personally irrational actions, the agent plays a central role. Either significantly increased risks of harm to the agent, or actual or expected harm to him, are essential. No action is objectively irrational without at least a significantly increased risk of harm to the agent. No action is personally irrational unless the agent believes or knows, or should believe or know, that he himself will suffer at least a significantly increased risk of harm. Causing harm to others is irrational only if it causes, or involves a significantly increased risk of, harm to the agent. Harming someone simply for revenge, not for some psychological or social benefit to himself or others, when the agent knows it is quite likely he will be caught and punished, is irrational. If a person who cares for someone else knows that causing harm to her causes him to suffer himself, then causing harm to her may be irrational. This kind of irrational action is not uncommon. People who love each other sometimes become angry at each other and act so as to harm the other person even though both know, or should know, that the suffering of the other person will cause them to suffer, and no one will benefit at all. Such actions are both objectively and personally irrational.

Concentration on harm to the agent, which is an essential feature of an irrational action, may lead some to the view that rationality is essentially egoistic. That would be a mistake. It is true that if the agent is not even significantly increasing his risk of being harmed, then his action cannot be irrational. Even harming others when doing so does not significantly increase his own risk of being harmed is not irrational. However, it does not follow that if the agent harms himself without thereby avoiding some other harm or without gaining any benefit for himself, then his action cannot be rational. Acting in order to avoid harms or gain benefits for others can make harming oneself rational. Everyone agrees that it is irrational for a person to harm herself without anyone avoiding a harm or gaining a benefit, but it is not irrational for a person to harm herself if she can thereby prevent greater harms to others. Even a person who gives up his life to save many others is not acting irrationally, let alone a person who simply gives up goods in order to help others avoid serious harms.

Reasons versus Motives

Much confusion has resulted from not distinguishing between reasons for an action, which can justify performing an action that would otherwise be irrational, and motives for an action, which provide part of the explanation for that action. "Reason" is often used as a synonym for "motive," but although this use of "reason" is an ordinary use, I do not use "reason" in this sense. I make a clear distinction between facts that can make an otherwise irrational action rational, and beliefs that explain why an action, rational or irrational, is done. Objective reasons are facts, which may not even be known to the agent and hence cannot serve as motives. Furthermore, reasons, either objective or personal, are limited to considerations about harms to be avoided or goods to be gained. Motives, including unconscious motives, are not so limited. Motives are related solely to an explanation of an action. Although they serve to make an action understandable, they need do nothing to show that the action is either objectively or personally rational. Objective reasons that are unknown to the agent are not related to motives at all. Objective reasons that are known to the agent become personal reasons, so that they can serve as motives. If the facts that are known to the agent concern avoidance of harm to himself, then it is irrational not to be motivated by them to some degree, even though that motivation may be overridden by the motivation to prevent harm to others. However, if these facts concern avoidance of harm or promoting of benefits to others, it is not irrational not to be motivated at all by them.

Although any fact that is an objective reason, if known, can serve as a motive, the reverse is not true; not all motives are beliefs about facts that are objective reasons. That an action will hurt someone is sometimes a motive for doing it, but it is never a reason for doing it; that is, it can never make an otherwise irrational action rational. The only facts that are reasons for an action are facts about the action helping someone (including oneself) to avoid or prevent (avoidable) death, pain, disability, loss of freedom, or loss of pleasure, or helping someone (including oneself) to gain or increase consciousness, ability, freedom, or pleasure. These facts about the action are the only basic objective reasons, and any other fact that counts as a reason is a reason because of its relationship to these facts. If any of these facts become known to a person, then they become beliefs that are personal reasons. If this knowledge motivates him, then these beliefs are motives as well as personal reasons. If adequate, they make an otherwise personally irrational action rational.

Objective reasons for acting are facts, but personal reasons for acting are beliefs. When we say, "There is a reason," we are talking about objective reasons. This is probably the ordinary use of the term "reason." When we say, "She has a reason," we may be saying that she knows some fact that is a reason, or we may be talking about personal reasons. "Personal reason" is a technical phrase, and I use it to refer to rational beliefs about facts that are objective reasons, whether or not those beliefs motivate the agent.[16] Only beliefs about harms avoided or benefits gained from an action are personal reasons for that action. However, if such beliefs are irrational, they are not reasons, although they can still be motives. A person who rationally believes that there is a fact that is an objective reason for acting has a personal reason for acting even if this belief does not motivate him at all. However, personal reasons that do not motivate a person cannot justify, that is, make personally rational, an otherwise personally irrational action. Only when the personal reason is a motive would we say that the personal reason for doing an otherwise personally irrational action made it personally rational to do it. This could explain why people often do not distinguish between reasons and motives.

The personal rationality of an act does not depend solely on the rational motivating beliefs of the agent; it also depends on what the agent should believe. If an agent acts, without a motivating personal reason for doing so, in a way that he should know will risk seriously harming himself, he is acting irrationally, even if he does not believe that his action will have that effect. But in order to justify an otherwise personally irrational action, a person normally must have a motivating personal reason for his action. If someone should know that his action will cause him some harm and has no motivating personal reason for doing it, his action is personally irrational even if he does not believe that he is harming himself. However, if a person acts to harm himself and should know that his action will avoid some harm or gain some benefit for himself or someone else, but he does not have this belief or it does not motivate him, then his action is still personally irrational. Although personal motivating reasons for acting must normally be conscious beliefs, desires for doing those actions that are commonly believed to have beneficial consequences are regarded as providing personal reasons for the person to do the act even if he has no conscious belief about these consequences.

All Reasons Have Justifying Force

The facts that can make an otherwise irrational action rational are facts about the avoidance of harms or the gaining of benefits from the action with regard to anyone. Unlike the facts that can make an action irrational, they are not limited to facts about the harms and benefits to the agent of the action. Although it is only facts about the agent suffering some harm that can make an action irrational, facts about anyone avoiding harms or gaining benefits can make an otherwise irrational action rational. Harming oneself for no reason is acting irrationally and counts as a symptom of a mental disorder. If such actions are quite serious and done very often, the person is not regarded as responsible for his actions. Harming others for no reason but with no increase in the chances of suffering harm oneself is acting immorally but not irrationally and does not count as a symptom of a mental disorder. Even if such actions are quite serious and done very often, the person is still regarded as responsible for his actions.

Rationality is a hybrid concept; harm to the agent is necessary for an action to be irrational, whereas avoidance of harm or gaining of benefits for anyone are reasons and can make an otherwise irrational action rational. The justifying force of a reason is completely determined by the amount of harm avoided or benefit gained, and it is irrelevant who avoids the harm or gains the benefit. Being able to justify, that is, to make an otherwise irrational action rational, is the essential feature of a reason. But if a reason has only justifying force, it is not irrational not to act on it, even if there are no opposing reasons. All reasons have justifying force, but only those reasons that concern avoiding or preventing harm to the agent have requiring force; that is, in the absence of opposing reasons, it is irrational not to act on them.

It is irrational for a person to take a 50 percent risk of losing his arm to get rid of an irritating wart on his finger. It is probably even irrational for him to take a 50 percent risk of losing his finger to get rid of the wart on it. It is not irrational for a person to take a 50 percent risk of losing his finger, or even to take a 50 percent risk of losing his arm, to save another person's life, even a person he does not know. Some people are more motivated to risk their arms or fingers to get rid of an irritating wart than they are to save the life of someone they do not know, but that is irrelevant to whether saving a person's life is a better or stronger justifying reason, that is, has more justifying force, than getting rid of a wart. That saving a stranger's life justifies risking losing your arm, whereas getting rid of an irritating wart does not, shows that the justifying force of a reason is determined by the otherwise irrational actions that it can make rational, not by how much it motivates a person, even a rational person, to act.

With respect to justifying, one reason is better or has more force than another if it can make rational every otherwise irrational action that the latter can make rational plus others besides. If nothing else is involved, relieving a serious pain has more justifying force than relieving a less serious pain. Avoiding five years in prison has more force than avoiding one year in prison. If rational persons disagree about whether one reason can make more otherwise irrational actions rational than another reason, then neither reason is better or has more justifying force. This will often happen when different kinds of harms are involved. One person may hold that avoiding death can make more otherwise irrational actions rational than avoiding permanent total physical disability with the associated suffering, whereas another person may hold the opposite. Both agree that preventing a more serious harm is a better reason than preventing a less serious harm, but they disagree about which is the more serious harm.

The primary role of reasons is to justify doing otherwise irrational actions. We need reasons only when our actions would be irrational without them. Of course, there may be objective reasons for an action that would not be objectively irrational even if there were no objective reasons for doing it. We can also have personal reasons for an action that would not be personally irrational even if we had no personal reasons for doing it. We do not need objective or personal reasons for most of the actions that we perform, although there can be objective reasons and we can have personal reasons for acting even when they are not needed. A person needs no reason for taking a walk on a nice summer day, but he can have several different reasons for doing so. One of those reasons might be that walking is good for his health; another might simply be that he will enjoy taking a walk.

Although all facts and beliefs that are reasons are facts and beliefs that can make otherwise irrational actions rational, some facts and beliefs, those that concern the agent suffering some harm, are such that, unless there are contrary reasons, it is also irrational not to act on them. In the absence of contrary reasons it is objectively irrational to act in a way that will result in your suffering some harm, and it is personally irrational to act in a way that you believe or should know will result in your suffering some harm. All reasons have justifying force, but reasons that involve avoiding harm to oneself are reasons that have not only a justifying force but also a requiring force.[17] The relative weights of the requiring force and the justifying force of these reasons (those involving avoiding harm to oneself) are the same; if one of these reasons has more justifying force than another, it also has more requiring force.

However, some reasons, those facts and beliefs that involve avoiding harms and gaining benefits for others for whom one has no concern, have only justifying force and have no requiring force. The justifying force of the fact that my action will save many people's lives is stronger than any fact about what harms I will avoid or benefits I will gain. That my action will save many people's lives makes rational any otherwise irrational act that any fact about avoiding harms or gaining benefits for myself will make rational and some others besides. However, the fact that my action will save many people's lives has no requiring force. If I do not act so as to save many people's lives simply because I do not care about them, that does not make my inaction irrational. (However, it does indicate a significant moral vice.) Although it is rational to refuse to save many people's lives in order to avoid a significant harm to myself, this is not because avoiding a significant harm to myself has greater justifying force than saving many people's lives but because saving many people's lives has no requiring force.

Only those reasons that concern harm to the agent have justifying force and requiring force. Not only can these reasons justify doing an otherwise irrational action, but in the absence of other reasons, the presence of these reasons can make it irrational not to do the action. All other reasons have no requiring force, but their justifying force can be as strong or stronger than the justifying and requiring force of those reasons that have both forces. Failure to recognize that not all reasons have both justifying force and requiring force allows people to put forward the following plausible sounding but confused account of a rational action: *a rational action is one that is based on the best reasons*, that is, those that have the most force.

On this account, in which "rational" means "rationally required," it is rationally required to act on the reasons with the most force. But once it is recognized that one reason can have more requiring force than another while the latter can have more justifying force, it is clear that the definition is confused. Does "based on the best reasons" mean reasons with the greatest justifying force or those with the greatest requiring force? Neither answer is satisfactory. It is not rationally required to act on reasons with the greatest requiring force if there are contrary reasons with greater justifying force. But it is also not rationally required to act on reasons with the greatest justifying force unless those reasons also have requiring force. Not acting on reasons with great justifying force but no requiring force, for no reason at all, is not acting irrationally. Objective reasons for helping someone can have great justifying force, but even though I am aware of the relevant facts, failing to help that person simply because I do not want to do so is not acting irrationally.

Distinguishing between the justifying force of a reason and its requiring force explains why in almost any conflict between self-interest and morality it is rationally allowed to act in either way. When morality conflicts with self-interest, there are always reasons for acting morally that are of equal or greater justifying force than the reasons of self-interest. However, reasons of self-interest are always of greater requiring force than the reasons for acting morally. To accept the claim that morality provides reasons with greater requiring force than reasons of self-interest do would result in irrationality no longer being the fundamental evaluative and normative concept. Many rational persons advocate to people for whom they are concerned, including themselves, that they not act as morality requires when acting immorally provides them with personal benefits without their suffering any harm. Even more would advocate not acting morally if acting morally would result in their suffering any significant harm. However, many other rational persons would advocate to those for whom they are concerned, including themselves, that they act as morality requires, or as it encourages, even when they would suffer significant harm by doing so. If rationality and irrationality are taken as the fundamental normative concepts, in a conflict between morality and self-interest, it cannot be rationally required to act in either way. Rather, it must be rationally allowed to act in both ways.

⁘
Reasons and Desires

Objective reasons for an action are facts, and these same facts are objective reasons for wanting to do the action. The objective reasons for a person taking a walk, that it is good for his health and that he will enjoy it, are also objective reasons for his wanting to take a walk. The personal reasons for his taking a walk, that he believes it is good for his health and that he will enjoy it, are also personal reasons for his wanting to take a walk. Of course, a person needs no reasons for wanting to take a walk, but if he did, wanting to take a walk would not provide a reason to take a walk or to want to take a walk.

It is sometimes claimed that the desires of the agent, at least those that are rational, provide objective reasons for acting. Perhaps it is thought that the fact that the agent has a desire is a reason for acting to satisfy that desire. If satisfying a rational desire significantly increases the probability of pleasure, or failing to satisfy a rational desire significantly increases the probability of displeasure, then having a desire is an objective reason for acting to satisfy it. The fact that one significantly increases the probability of gaining pleasure from satisfying a desire or significantly increases the probability of suffering some displeasure from not satisfying it are objective reasons for satisfying that desire. But satisfying a desire is not a basic objective reason; it is only a reason insofar as it is related to the basic objective reasons of gaining pleasure and avoiding displeasure.[18]

Desires are not basic reasons. Considered by themselves, they cannot make an otherwise objectively irrational action rational, or an otherwise personally irrational action rational. Of course, most of the things I want to do, do not have harmful consequences for myself, so I do not need any reasons for doing them. Although it is usually quite rational to do what I desire to do, this is not because desiring to do it is a reason for doing it but because I do not need any reasons for doing it. No irrational action can be made rational simply by a desire to do it. If an action is going to result in my being blinded, neither my irrational desire to be blinded nor any rational desire that does not involve avoiding harms or gaining benefits can make that action rational. Suppose I want to look directly at the sun and I am told that doing so will result in blindness. It may be that accepting the belief that looking at the sun will result in blindness takes away my desire to look directly at the sun. I may feel neither disappointment nor displeasure at not satisfying that desire. However, perhaps I still have the desire to do so. If I would feel some disappointment or displeasure at not satisfying my desire to look directly at the sun, then I do have an objective reason for looking directly at the sun, although, given that it will result in blindness, it would not be an adequate reason.

Adequate Reasons

Not all reasons are adequate to make acting on a particular otherwise irrational desire rational. That I would be disappointed by not looking directly at the sun is not an adequate objective reason for looking at the sun if doing so will result in my becoming blind. It is not even an adequate reason for looking at the sun if doing so will result in only a 50 percent risk of becoming blind. A much stronger reason is needed in order to be an adequate reason for doing something that will result in becoming blind or a 50 percent risk of becoming blind. That my action will save the lives of several people would be an adequate reason for looking at the sun. Within limits, determining what reasons are adequate for a particular otherwise irrational act is a matter on which rational persons disagree. This should be clear from the fact that it is rational to rank harms and benefits in many different ways.

That what one person regards as an adequate reason for suffering some harm would not be regarded by another as an adequate reason does not mean that one person is motivated by a fact that the second person would not be motivated by. Rather, it means that the first person regards someone who suffers the harm for that reason to be acting rationally and the second person does not. There is not complete agreement among rational persons about the ranking of harms and benefits, so there will not be complete agreement among rational persons about the adequacy of a given reason for suffering a particular harm. This means that there will not be complete agreement among rational persons about the rationality, either objective or personal, of some acts. In order for irrationality to be the fundamental evaluative or normative concept, it cannot be applied to any action that any significant number of otherwise rational persons would advocate to people for whom they are concerned.

If only one person would advocate to people for whom he cares that they do some self-harming action for the reason under consideration, that person is not regarded as a rational person. If only a very small number of people would advocate to people for whom they care that they do some self-harming action for the reason under consideration, that small number of people are also not regarded as rational. However, any reason that any significant number of otherwise rational persons appraises as adequate is objectively adequate. When a person learns that a significant number of otherwise rational persons rank the harms and benefits differently than he does, and so appraise as adequate a reason that he appraises as inadequate, this should change his view about the rationality of the resulting action. He should acknowledge that, despite his personal view, the action is objectively rational. This seemingly unlikely sequence of events is in fact a common occurrence in medicine.

Physicians often rank death as a much worse evil than suffering pain; thus, they often appraise a patient's decision to discontinue a painful life-prolonging treatment as irrational. They do not regard the avoidance of that amount of pain as an adequate reason for dying sooner than one would by continuing the treatment. Nonetheless, when informed that many patients rank avoiding the pain and discomfort as an adequate reason for discontinuing treatment, they do not try to overrule the patient's decision to discontinue treatment but rather treat avoiding the pain and discomfort as an adequate reason for discontinuing the life-prolonging treatment. This does not mean that physicians come to be motivated to discontinue life-prolonging treatment to avoid the pain, only that they come to regard discontinuing such treatment as rationally allowed. (See flow charts on rationality on page 151.)

▚ Rationality, Morality, and Self-Interest

That rationality does not resolve the conflicts that sometimes arise between morality and self-interest is quite disappointing to many philosophers. Starting at least as far back as Plato, philosophers have tried to reconcile morality and self-interest or to show that when morality conflicts with self-interest, rationality requires acting morally. However, morality does sometimes conflict with self-interest and when this happens rationality does not require acting morally. Rationality does not even always require acting morally when morality and self-interest require doing the same action. In fact, the most serious immoral actions are usually not done from motives of self-interest. Rather, nationalism, racism, and religion have resulted in far more morally unjustified harm being caused than has self-interest. Furthermore, such actions are usually rationally allowed. It is also rationally allowed to suffer some harm to avoid greater harm for others for whom one is concerned even when these actions are immoral. A person can cause himself harm in order to prevent greater harm to people for whom he is concerned, even though he is causing even greater harm to people for whom he is not concerned. Acting altruistically is not necessarily acting morally, a conclusion that is surprising to many people because too much attention is given to self-interest as the primary opponent of morality.

Contrary to what is widely believed, not only do people sometimes act both immorally and against their own self-interest to benefit those for whom they are concerned, but such actions are often not irrational. For those who want to justify acting morally, this is an extremely disappointing conclusion. Not only does rationality not require acting morally when acting morally conflicts with self-interest, but even when self-interest and morality require acting in the same way, rationality need not require people to act in that way. Any modification of the concept of rationality to make it require always acting morally, even when acting morally is in one's self-interest, results in rationality no longer being the fundamental evaluative and normative concept.

Making it rationally required to act morally when there is conflict between acting morally and acting to benefit those for whom she is concerned results in its making sense for a moral agent to ask, "Why should I act rationally?" Parents are not acting irrationally when they act to benefit their children even when such action is both immoral and contrary to their own self-interest. If it were irrational, that would result in a significant number of rational persons advocating to those for whom they are concerned that they act irrationally, thus depriving irrationality of its role as the fundamental normative concept. However, it is also not irrational to act morally when morality conflicts with self-interest or with the interests of those for whom one is concerned. It is not irrational to act morally when considering violating a moral rule that will benefit oneself or those one cares for and harm those for whom one has no concern. Unfortunately, it is also not irrational not to act morally in these circumstances. Stated generally, it is not irrational to be impartial when considering a violation of a moral rule, and it is also not irrational not to be impartial.

⠿
Impartiality

Impartiality has been so neglected by philosophers that it is not surprising that the brief characterizations of it have been so inadequate. Very good philosophers have said that impartiality is taking a God's-eye point of view or the point of view of the universe.[19] Since no one knows what such a point of view is, these remarks are useless. Further, they are completely mistaken about the nature of general impartiality. They are even mistaken about the kind of impartiality they are attempting to characterize, the kind of impartiality required by morality. It is not generally appreciated that it is impossible to talk about impartiality all by itself; impartiality presupposes a group with regard to which a person is impartial and a respect in which the person is impartial with regard to that group. Fathers often are impartial with regard to their own children with respect to spending time with them, but no father is impartial in that respect with regard to all children. The need for precision in characterizing acting impartially can be seen from the fact that a person can act impartially with regard to the same group in one respect but not in another. A teacher may act impartially with regard to all students in her class with respect to grading tests and papers and yet not act impartially with regard to them with respect to providing help to them or calling on them in class.

Similarly misleading is one of the most common characterizations of impartiality as treating like cases alike. This characterization confuses impartiality with consistency, as can be seen by considering the case of a disgruntled baseball umpire. This umpire believes that umpires are not appreciated, and so, while remaining within acceptable interpretations of the rules, he decides to change the way in which he calls balls and strikes by widening or shrinking the strike zone every fifteen minutes. He is completely unconcerned by how this affects either team or any batter or pitcher. Such an umpire might be suspected of partiality, but if he acts as I have described, that suspicion would be false. He is not a consistent umpire and so is not a good umpire, for umpiring requires consistency as well as impartiality, but he is still impartial.[20]

The following definition incorporates the realization that impartiality requires reference to a group with regard to which a person is impartial, and a respect in which he is impartial with regard to that group. *A is impartial in respect R with regard to group G if and only if A's actions in respect R are not influenced by which member(s) of G benefit or are harmed by these actions.*[21] Briefly, a person is impartial with regard to a group in a given respect if he does not favor any member of the group over any other member in that respect. This definition of impartiality needs to be supplemented when discussing moral impartiality, for impartiality with regard to a group of which one is a member requires that one make no special exceptions for oneself or others with regard to who can violate a moral rule. Moral impartiality still requires specifying both the group toward which and the respect in which impartiality is required.

People disagree about whether morality requires impartiality with regard to any group larger than all moral agents.[22] In particular, they disagree about whether fetuses or nonhuman animals such as dolphins or chimpanzees are included in that group. It is a mistake to think that the group with regard to which morality requires impartiality can be determined impartially, because all talk of impartiality presupposes that there is already a group with regard to which impartiality is required. It is not irrational not to be impartial in the way that morality requires, but people who are impartial with regard to a group consisting only of those of their own gender, race, religion, nationality, or ethnic group are sexist, racist, and so on, not moral. With respect to obeying moral rules, morality requires impartiality with regard to a group that includes at least all moral agents.

Because morality requires impartiality with regard to at least all moral agents, the respect in which morality requires impartiality must be a respect in which it is humanly possible to be impartial toward a group as large as all moral agents. Unless a person does not act on any moral ideals at all, it is not humanly possible for her to follow the moral ideals impartially with regard to all moral agents. No one can relieve pain and suffering with regard to all moral agents impartially. However, it is humanly possible to be impartial with regard to all moral agents when considering violating a moral rule. In fact, it is only when considering violating moral rules, for example, "Do not kill" and "Keep your promises," that morality requires impartiality. If your child needs a heart transplant, morality does not allow you to kill some other child in order to obtain a suitable heart. However, if two children fall out of a boat and one of them is your child, morality neither requires nor encourages that you be impartial in deciding which one to rescue first.[23]

⁑
Two Philosophical Attempts to Achieve Moral Impartiality

Kant's Categorical Imperative and Rawls's veil of ignorance are both viewed so favorably because both seem to embody impartiality, an essential feature of morality. It is true that if someone acted only on those maxims that she would will to be a universal law of nature, she would necessarily be impartial. It is also true that if it were possible for someone to go under Rawls's veil, which it is not, she could not help but be impartial. However, although going under Rawls's veil of ignorance results in impartiality, it allows for a moral system that might require facts that not all rational persons are aware of. Adopting the blindfold of justice is not only sufficient to guarantee impartiality but also guarantees that no facts not known to all moral agents will be used in formulating or supporting the moral system. As long as a person does not use any particular facts about herself that would allow her to design the moral system to favor herself or those for whom she cares, the moral system will be impartial with regard to all moral agents. Going under Rawls's veil of ignorance guarantees not only impartiality but also unanimity. However, impartiality does not require unanimity. Although actual persons can disagree about whether a maxim satisfies Kant's Categorical Imperative—so that by itself, the Categorical Imperative does not guarantee unanimity—combined with Kant's account of the rational self, it does. Moreover, to satisfy the Categorical Imperative, it is required that a person will that everyone in the circumstances being considered act in the same way.

Two impartial basketball referees can differ in the way that they call fouls, yet both remain impartial. One referee may prefer a game with minimum bodily contact and hence call more fouls, whereas the other may prefer a faster game with fewer interruptions and hence call fewer fouls. But both may be completely impartial, being completely uninfluenced by which team or which players are benefited or harmed by the way that they call fouls. Rawls's veil of ignorance, although it does guarantee impartiality, misleadingly suggests that impartiality requires unanimity. Rawls requires unanimity because of another feature of his theory, namely, his formal account of rationality. He has no way of limiting rational disagreement once any disagreement is allowed. Impartiality does not require unanimity. If it did, then a person who admitted that United States Supreme Court justices were rational and had equal knowledge of the relevant facts and the law would be required to hold that any split decision showed that at least one side was not being impartial.

Like Rawls's veil of ignorance, Kant's Categorical Imperative not only guarantees impartiality but also requires unanimity. It is true that if a person acts only on those maxims that he wills that everyone act on, he would be acting impartially, but it is not true that if he does not act on such maxims, he would not be acting impartially. It is sufficient for a person to be acting impartially if he acts only on those maxims that he would be willing for everyone to know that they are allowed to act on. This is sufficient to show that he is not making any special exceptions for himself. Because of the way that Kant formulates the first version of the Categorical Imperative, it seems to lead to unacceptable conclusions. Acting on the correct account of impartiality allows a person to act on the maxim "In order to be polite, never be the last to leave a party," but acting on such a maxim would violate Kant's Categorical Imperative.[24] Kant makes the additional mistake of requiring all of our actions to conform to the Categorical Imperative rather than just those actions that involve violations of moral rules.

Both Kant and Rawls, like most philosophers, are primarily, if not solely, concerned with the kind of impartiality that is required by morality. However, it is not possible to provide an adequate account of moral impartiality unless one has an adequate account of impartiality itself. There have been few, if any, serious attempts to provide a philosophical account of impartiality itself. Evidence for this is that it is and has been commonly accepted as a trivial truth that impartiality requires treating like cases alike. However, this "trivial truth" simply confuses impartiality with consistency, as is shown by the example of the baseball umpire discussed in the previous section.

Impartiality is a more complex concept than it seems to be at first glance. One of the most confusing features of impartiality is that it makes no sense to characterize a person simply as acting impartially. We may think that this makes sense because we forget that we are assuming that we know in what respect the person is acting impartially and with regard to what group. Acting impartially does not guarantee acting in a morally acceptable way if the group with regard to which a person acts impartially is not the appropriate group. For example, suppose a person acts impartially with regard to all males applying for a job, whereas he is supposed to act impartially with regard to all persons applying for the job. Acting impartially with regard to all males is not morally acceptable. Nor is a person who acts impartially with regard to all those with whom he interacts in picking the next victim of his criminal activity acting in a morally acceptable way. The claim that impartiality is a moral virtue makes sense only if we assume that both the group toward which and the respect in which the person is acting impartially are morally appropriate.

::

Justifying Moral Impartiality

Why morality requires impartiality with respect to the moral rules

In the description of common morality, I pointed out that morality requires impartiality only with respect to obeying the moral rules, not with respect to following the moral ideals. It is not simply an accident that all of the moral rules are formulated, or can be formulated, as prohibitions. If I do not violate the rules prohibiting killing, causing pain, disabling, depriving of freedom, depriving of pleasure, deceiving or cheating, I do not violate them with regard to anyone. I obey them impartially. Although not quite so obvious, if I do not violate the rules requiring keeping promises, obeying the law, and doing my duty, it is also true that I do not break a promise, disobey a law, or neglect a duty with regard to anyone. Complete obedience to these rules is necessarily impartial obedience, but complete obedience is not what rational persons, under the conditions in which they would all endorse morality, favor.

The moral rules set limits on what a person is allowed to do no matter what his goals are. A person who wants to act morally does not often need to violate them. However, sometimes the moral rules conflict, or following a moral ideal conflicts with obeying a moral rule. Contrary to what Kant suggests, it must be possible to be impartial with respect to the moral rules with regard to all moral agents, even in those cases where a person violates a rule. A person is impartial with respect to a moral rule with regard to all moral agents even when she is violating it, if she does so justifiably. If, when deciding whether to violate a rule, a person is not influenced by which particular persons are harmed or benefited by that violation, she is impartial with respect to that moral rule with regard to all moral agents, whether she violates it or not. The way in which a person demonstrates this impartiality is by violating a rule only if she would be willing for everyone to know that they are allowed to violate that rule in these same circumstances. She would be willing for everyone to know this only if she estimated that better consequences would result if everyone knew this than if everyone knew they were not allowed to violate the rule in those circumstances. Using only rationally required beliefs, all rational persons who are justifying morality to others would not favor that people obey a moral rule when every rational person would be willing for everyone to know that they are allowed to violate that rule in these same circumstances, that is, when every rational person would estimate that better consequences would result if everyone knew this.

It is important in this context to point out that what counts as the same circumstances, or the same kind of violation, must be described in a way that could be understood by all moral agents. Requiring that violations be described using only the morally relevant features prevents a person from describing the violation in a way that would bias the moral system in order to benefit himself and those for whom he is concerned. By limiting justifiable violations in this way, people are prevented from making special exceptions for themselves and their friends. The two-step procedure for justifying violations—describing the act using only morally relevant features and considering whether one would be willing for everyone to know that they are allowed to violate that rule in these same circumstances—ensures impartiality with respect to the moral rules. The second step resembles Kant's Categorical Imperative, but it is not distorted by the metaphysical requirements that make the Categorical Imperative inadequate. Rather, it is based on the estimate of the consequences that would result if everyone knows that they are allowed to break the rule. Furthermore, the explicit list of the morally relevant features that are used in determining what counts as the same kind of violation removes the subjectivity that plagues anyone who attempts to formulate the maxims which are supposed to be tested by the Categorical Imperative.

Contrary to Kant, morality requires impartiality only with respect to obeying a moral rule. Rational persons rightly regard enforcing justified impartial obedience to the moral rules as preventing far more harm than it causes. Making persons liable to punishment (e.g., by enacting laws or allowing for suits for damages) for nontrivial, unjustified violations of the moral rules does deprive persons of freedom, but it significantly reduces the risks that a person will suffer more serious harms from the unjustified violations of the moral rules by others. Even with regard to weakly justified violations, Hobbes has provided a strong argument that people gain far more than they lose by agreeing that these kinds of violations should be liable to punishment.[25] However, rational persons would not agree that failure to act on the moral ideals impartially should make one liable to punishment. Many would regard this as giving up more control over their lives than is warranted by the reduction in the risk of suffering harm.

Rational persons are aware that whereas everyone is always morally required to obey a moral rule unless violating it can be publicly allowed, this kind of requirement is pointless and counterproductive with regard to the moral ideals.[26] Not only is it impossible to act on the moral ideals all of the time, but even when acting on them, it is pointless and counterproductive to act on them impartially. Further, as Mill points out, acting impartially is "more likely to be blamed than applauded" when acting in that way is not required by a moral rule or a duty.[27] The realization that impartiality is neither encouraged nor required when following moral ideals removes most of the objections to the claim that morality requires impartiality. The rest of the objections are removed by remembering that, because the relationship between the victim and the violator is one of the morally relevant features of the violation, it is completely compatible with obeying the moral rules impartially to take this relationship into account.

The two-step procedure for justifying violations not only requires describing a violation in a way that all rational persons can understand but also requires estimating the consequences of everyone knowing that this kind of violation is allowed. If all rational persons consider these consequences to be better than the consequences of everyone knowing that this kind of violation is not allowed, then all rational persons would favor allowing the rule to be violated. If they all consider the consequences of not allowing the rule to be violated to be better than the consequences of allowing the rule to be violated, then all rational persons would favor not allowing the rule to be violated. Rational persons naturally favor that public system which has the better consequences.

However, they are aware that rational persons, even when using only rationally required beliefs, can still disagree. When rational persons disagree about whether the consequences of publicly allowing a violation are better than the consequences of not publicly allowing a violation, they will not agree on what should be done. This is why morality does not resolve every moral problem. The almost universal failure of philosophers to acknowledge that morality does not provide a unique correct answer to every moral question about what ought to be done is one of the causes of moral skepticism. It is not generally recognized that disagreement on the correct answer to a controversial question is compatible with complete agreement that 99 percent of the possible answers are incorrect. It is also compatible with complete agreement on the answers to 99 percent of the moral questions.

The group with regard to which morality requires impartiality

Understanding the nature of impartiality makes clear that not only must the respect in which morality requires impartiality be specified but also the group with regard to which morality requires impartiality must be specified. It has been shown why all rational persons require impartiality with respect to obeying moral rules, and only in this respect. Only when considering violations of the moral rules does impartiality result in less overall evil being suffered. Attempting to follow moral ideals impartially would not have this result. However, this same kind of universal agreement does not obtain concerning the group with regard to which morality requires impartiality. On the contrary, within limits, rational persons disagree about the group with regard to which morality requires impartiality. The dispute over abortion is the clearest example of this disagreement, but there are also disagreements about whether some nonhuman animals belong in the group with regard to which morality requires impartiality.

The question "What is the group with regard to which morality requires impartiality?" seems to presuppose that there is agreement among all rational persons on the group with regard to which morality requires impartiality. But there is no such agreement. There is agreement on a similar sounding but completely different question: "To whom do the moral rules apply?" Common morality applies to all and only moral agents, those rational persons who know what is required and prohibited by the moral rules and can guide their behavior by their knowledge. However, although there is agreement concerning who is subject to moral judgment (namely, all moral agents), there is no agreement among these moral agents about who is impartially protected by the moral rules.

In addition to Kant's view that the moral rules impartially protect only moral agents and Bentham's view that all beings who can feel pain are impartially protected, there is the view that the moral rules impartially protect all potential moral agents, as well as all actual moral agents. It might even be possible to hold that the moral rules impartially protect all potentially sentient beings, as well as those who are actually sentient beings. No rational person would accept the Kantian view. They are all aware that they may cease to be moral agents and yet not be permanently unconscious. They would not want to lose their protection against unjustified causing of pain if that happened; therefore, they would include in the minimal group that is impartially protected by the moral rules all actual moral agents and all former moral agents who are conscious or who may regain consciousness. Although rational persons can be concerned with a much wider group, all rational persons are concerned with protecting themselves now and for as long as they are not permanently unconscious.

No rational person using only rationally required beliefs would hold that the moral rules protect a smaller group than the minimal group, for example, either just men or just women, or just people of a certain nationality or race or religion. This explains why everyone agrees that violating a moral rule without an adequate justification with regard to those moral agents who are not members of the included gender, nation, race, or religion is acting immorally. Holding that the moral rules impartially protect only those in some smaller group is to be a sexist, nationalist, racist, or religious fanatic. Such persons are using more than rationally required beliefs. But that there is agreement on the minimal group impartially protected by morality does not mean that there is agreement that moral rules impartially protect only those in the minimal group.

Almost everyone holds that morality also impartially protects some potential moral agents who are not yet actual moral agents, such as infants and small children. Rational persons know that, as parents, they might care for their children as much as, if not more than, they care for other moral agents, including themselves. No rational person cares for nonsentient beings as much or more than they care for moral agents, including themselves. It is not even clear that any rational person holds that morality impartially protects the maximum group, all potentially sentient beings. Although environmentalists seem to attach some moral weight to preserving the environment, to be a rational concern this has to be because of the environment's importance to sentient beings, though not necessarily human beings. No rational person thinks that protecting a world no sentient being will ever experience justifies anyone suffering any harm.[28] Furthermore, anyone who intentionally acts so as to cause harm to a moral agent rather than cause that same harm to a nonhuman animal is correctly regarded as acting immorally. No rational person regards a nonhuman's well-being as equally as important as his own well-being. Nonetheless, some people hold that morality does provide some protection to sentient nonhuman beings, especially mammals that have a high level of intelligence and social interaction.

Because morality must be understood by all those to whom it applies, the content of the moral system cannot be determined by beliefs that are not shared by all other rational persons. This means that no religious or scientific beliefs that are not shared by all normal adult human beings can be used. Everyone knows that parents often care for their children more than they care for other people, so it is not surprising that children would be included in the group that almost everyone would claim should be impartially protected. Pregnant women often have a protective attitude toward their fetuses. There would be universal agreement that the fetus is impartially protected from harm by everyone other than the pregnant woman. However, this would be the result of knowing that harming a fetus that the pregnant woman did not want harmed would be seriously harming the pregnant woman. Everyone holds that pregnant women are impartially protected by the moral rules. It is important to recognize that laws prohibiting abortion protect the fetus only from that person who has the closest relationship to it, the pregnant woman. Many of those who want fetuses to be included in the impartially protected group do so because of religious beliefs, but such beliefs are not allowed in determining the group that morality impartially protects because they are not shared by all rational persons. Nonetheless, a rational person need not have religious beliefs in order to want fetuses to be included in the group that is impartially protected. Given the close relationship between fetuses and infants, it is not considered irrational for a person to be as concerned for a fetus as for any moral agent.

Few, if any, rational persons who use only rationally required beliefs would extend the impartial protection of morality to any nonhuman animals. There are beliefs, some of which may even be rationally required (e.g., that some nonhuman animals feel pain), that are used to support the view that these sentient beings are impartially protected. But insofar as morality is that public system that all rational persons have adopted to protect themselves and those for whom they are concerned, nonhuman animals would not be impartially protected. Every increase in the group that is impartially protected decreases the freedom of those moral agents who are already in the impartially protected group. Although the fact that some nonhuman animals feel pain might lead many rational persons to want them protected, it does not follow that they would want them included in the group that is impartially protected. No moral agent who is driving a car and must choose between hitting a human being and hitting a nonhuman animal would think it morally appropriate to flip a coin in order to decide which to hit.

Morality requires that a person never violate a moral rule unless she would be willing for everyone to know that they are allowed to violate the rule in the same circumstances. Whether the being who is being harmed is included in the group that is impartially protected, or protected at all, is not one of the morally relevant features, because all of the morally relevant features are facts that apply when considering violating a rule with regard to anyone in the impartially protected group. There is no fact of the matter about whether fetuses are in the impartially protected group. Beyond moral agents and former moral agents, and possibly infants and children, the scope of morality, or who is included in the impartially protected group or a group that is at least partially protected by morality, is a source of moral disagreement, not a fact that can change one's moral judgment about a particular violation. The claim that morality requires impartiality with regard to all those who can suffer any harm is not a claim that most moral agents would accept, even though it is possible that some would.

Morality impartially protects all moral agents because no rational person using only rationally required beliefs would agree to endorse morality unless she were impartially protected by it. Moral agents would want themselves to be protected (e.g., would not want to be made to suffer pain unjustifiably) even if they cease to be moral agents, as long as they remain conscious. Thus, the minimal group impartially protected by morality includes not only actual moral agents but also former moral agents who are still conscious. Most rational persons will demand that the group be enlarged to include children who are not yet moral agents. Any enlargement beyond this would be quite controversial. There is no argument for enlarging the minimal group or for showing that it should not be enlarged that all rational persons would or should take to be conclusive. The fact that rational persons using only rationally required beliefs can disagree on which group is impartially protected by morality, and on how much those not in the impartially protected group should be protected, explains why abortion and the question about how morality requires animals to be treated are unresolvable questions.

Why Act Morally?

Although it is usually not rationally required to act morally, it is never irrational to act as morality encourages or requires. The reasons in favor of acting morally always have sufficient justifying force to make it rationally allowed to act morally. This may not satisfy those who want it to be rationally required to act morally; however, it is the best that can be done without distorting the relevant concepts of morality and rationality. The view that it is always irrational to act immorally has the counterintuitive result that many rational persons would advocate to those for whom they are concerned that they act irrationally. For example, some political campaign advisors suggest to the candidate that he should attempt to deceive the voters about some of his views. Thus, either irrationality would no longer be the fundamental evaluative and normative concept, or else the concept of morality would become completely distorted. It would no longer be immoral to violate a moral rule when no rational person would be willing for everyone to know that they were allowed to break the rule in the same morally relevant circumstances.

If it were ever irrational to act morally, the following inconsistency would result if there were any rational persons who were impartial with respect to obeying the moral rules with regard to all moral agents. If any action were both irrational and morally required, then all rational persons would have to advocate to all those for whom they are concerned not to do it, while all rational persons who are impartial with respect to obeying the moral rules with regard to all moral agents would have to advocate that they do it. It is implausible to claim that no rational person is impartial with respect to obeying the moral rules with regard to all moral agents, so although rationality cannot require acting morally, it does always allow acting as morality requires.

The desire to make it irrational to be immoral may explain why some people hold that morality requires belief in a special kind of God. Such a God could make it such that no one for whom a person is concerned ever benefits from an immoral act, and every immoral act is punished so severely that it would be irrational to act immorally. Without such a God, it is not possible to provide an answer to the question "Why should I act morally?" that provides reasons of sufficient requiring force that it would be irrational to act immorally. However, even without a God, it is always possible to provide reasons of sufficient justifying force that it is always rationally allowed to act morally. This is far different from claiming that it is always possible to provide a rational person with motives of sufficient strength to persuade him to act morally. It is not irrational to act immorally.

Rational persons who do not care about moral agents who are not known to them will not be persuaded to act morally when acting morally conflicts with their own self-interest or the interests of those for whom they are concerned, such as family and friends. Some rational persons are unconcerned with people who do not belong to their own ethnic, national, racial, or religious group. These people will not be motivated to act morally when their immoral actions harm only those not in their group and benefit people in their group. However, if an action is morally required or encouraged, there are always adequate reasons to do it. Anytime that it seems that acting morally requires adequate reasons and there are no adequate reasons, then some mistake has been made. If keeping a trivial promise requires suffering sufficiently great harm, then morality neither requires nor encourages keeping that promise. In these kinds of cases, all rational persons would publicly allow breaking the promise. Acting morally often does not require any reasons because acting morally often is not acting contrary to one's self-interest. Indeed, reasons of self-interest often support acting morally.

The basic reason for acting morally is to avoid causing harm to other people. All unjustified violations of the first five rules cause, or significantly increase the risk of, harm to others. This reason for acting morally is so obvious that the question "Why should I act morally?" is not usually asked with respect to the first five moral rules. However, a particularly uncaring person might ask, "Why should I avoid causing harm to others?" There are all sorts of answers that can be given to this question, but none of them are likely to motivate the callous person to act morally. It is not rationally required to avoid causing harm to others. As pointed out earlier, avoiding causing harm to others has great justifying force but no requiring force. One might try to provide answers with requiring force, such as "The person you hurt will try to hurt you," "If you get caught, you will be punished," or "God will punish you for harming others." However, sometimes these answers will not carry much weight: the victim will not know who hurt him or cannot retaliate, your chances of getting caught are close to nil, and there is little or no evidence to believe in the existence of a God who punishes all immoral behavior.

The fact that he will harm someone by acting immorally may not motivate a callous person not to act in that way, but that fact is still a reason for not violating any of the first five moral rules. However, many unjustified violations of the second five rules do not seem to cause, or significantly increase the risk of, harm to others. It is with regard to these kinds of unjustified violations that it is most common to hear caring people sincerely ask, "Why should I act morally?" Normally, the reasons for acting morally will have greater justifying force than any conflicting reasons for acting in one's self-interest or in the interests of those for whom one is concerned. Criminal activity usually involves a loss to the victim, avoiding which has far greater justifying force than the benefits gained by the criminal. However, that is not always the case. Sometimes the criminal, especially in a nonviolent crime, gains more than any person loses. Sophisticated computer crimes where fractions of a cent are transferred from the accounts of many victims to the account of the criminal can, if enough people are involved, provide great benefits to the criminal and negligible losses to anyone else. Some cases of deceiving and cheating can benefit the deceiver or cheater without harming anyone else at all.

Awareness of immoral behavior that does not appear to have harmful effects on anyone may make it seem that the reasons supporting acting morally do not always have equal or greater justifying force than the reasons supporting immoral behavior. Limiting consideration to the direct effects of a single act has the result that the reasons for acting morally sometimes do not have as much justifying force as the reasons for acting immorally. No acceptable moral theory can have as one of its implications that it is sometimes irrational to act as one is morally required to act. Awareness of all of this provides an incentive for holding that the morally required act is always the one with the best consequences in the particular case.[29] However, this yields counterintuitive results, such as that it is morally required to cheat when you gain by doing so and no one else loses, even though no rational person would be willing for everyone to know that cheating in the morally relevant circumstances is allowed.

If the reasons for acting as morality requires are always going to have a justifying force equal to or greater than the justifying or requiring force of the reasons for acting immorally, it is necessary to take into account some of the indirect reasons for acting morally. One indirect reason concerns the effect of unjustified violations on the strength of the moral rules. Normally, the more often people unjustifiably violate a moral rule, the more likely it is that other people will violate moral rules unjustifiably. The more often that moral rules are unjustifiably violated, the greater the risk of harm being suffered. Thus, the argument concludes that the indirect reasons for acting as morality requires always have a justifying force that is as strong as any reason for acting immorally. Although this argument is plausible, it does not seem to me to be conclusive. It does not account for those cases in which a person violates a moral rule secretly.

A better argument for the position that the indirect reasons for acting morally always have sufficient force to be adequate involves the character of the agent. Breaking a moral rule when you would not want everyone to know that they are allowed to break that moral rule in the same circumstances is to act arrogantly. Arrogance is incompatible with the impartiality required by morality. Someone who acts arrogantly, even when he has good reason to believe that the direct reasons for acting immorally have greater justifying and requiring force than the direct reasons for acting morally, is far more likely to act arrogantly when he has no good reason to believe that the reasons for acting immorally have greater requiring force than the justifying reasons for acting morally. Such a person does not recognize his own fallibility. His lack of the appropriate humility makes it far more likely that he will act immorally when more harm would be caused by his immoral action than by his acting morally. This argument seems to me to be considerably stronger than the argument concerning the effect of immoral action on the strength of the moral rules.

When considering only the direct reasons for a particular act, it is extremely difficult, if not impossible, to show that the reasons for acting morally always have as much force or more force than the reasons for acting immorally. Perhaps it was the recognition of this fact that led many philosophers to try to answer the question "Why be moral?" rather than the question "Why act morally?" These two questions are not the same. The first is about why one should be a moral person, that is, have the moral virtues, not why one should act morally in a particular case. The arguments for being a moral person are far stronger than the arguments for acting morally in any particular case. There are reasons of much stronger justifying force for being a moral person than for being an immoral person.

In a decent society, one where most people act morally most of the time, parents who are concerned solely with the happiness and success of their children would bring them up to be moral rather than to be immoral. Moral persons, those with all the moral virtues, are far more likely to be happy and successful than those who are immoral, even than those who can seem moral while acting immorally. In most societies, being discovered to be an immoral person always has bad consequences, and as Hobbes pointed out, it is not reasonable to think that you will not be found out. But even if one is not found out, being immoral results in the frustration of wanting to act immorally but not being able to do so without fear of being discovered. I am not claiming that the reasons for being moral have more requiring force than the reasons for being immoral, but if one is living in a decent society, this is not an implausible claim. In a decent society, it may even be rationally required for parents who love their children to bring them up to be moral persons. But even if the reasons for being a moral person do not have more requiring force than the reasons for being an immoral person, they have far more justifying force. Far less harm is caused by a moral person than by an immoral person.

⁛
Morality as an Informal Public System

Morality is a guide to conduct, so it is natural to think that it should provide guidance about how persons should act in every moral situation. And it does. But providing guidance is not the same as providing a unique correct answer to every question about how a person should act in every moral situation. Morality always provides guidance because it always provides limits to the morally acceptable ways of acting. However, this is not always of much practical value, because generally those limits on the ways of acting are already known. People who want to act morally may want morality to provide guidance in all controversial cases. They may want morality to tell them how to act when they are not clear about the way in which they morally ought to act. They may express their concern by saying that what they want to know is "What is the morally right way to act?" However, if "the morally right way to act" means the way that all fully informed, impartial rational persons would agree that all persons morally ought to act, in some situations there will not be any act that is the morally right way to act.

Although there is not always only one morally acceptable way of acting, in every moral situation there are always morally better and morally worse ways of acting. However, there is not always a unique morally best way of acting. Unlike law, morality is not a formal system that has procedures for determining a unique correct answer in every case. Morality is an informal system, like a neighborhood game, in which there is agreement on how the game is to be played in the overwhelming majority of cases, but in which there are some cases about which there is some limited disagreement. In these disputed cases, the players may reach some negotiated compromise, make an ad hoc decision, or simply stop playing. When it becomes important for a game to continue to a conclusion, as in professional sports, the game becomes a formal system with judges or umpires who are given the authority to make the final decisions.

Although morality is a public system that applies to all rational persons who understand what kinds of actions it prohibits, requires, discourages, encourages, and allows, and who can guide their behavior by their understanding, it is still an informal system. Unlike other informal systems that can break down if disputes cannot be settled, morality will continue even if there are some unresolvable disagreements. These disagreements always occur within an area of larger agreement, and morality imposes limitations on the way in which the disagreements may be settled. However, when there is an unresolvable disagreement, it is sometimes necessary to arrive at a decision about how to act. It is for this reason that law and politics supplement morality. When people need to decide what to do when confronted with a morally unresolvable issue, the issue is appropriately, though often only temporarily, settled by legal or political means, but the issue remains morally unresolved. This is what has happened with the abortion issue.

The law can prohibit behavior that, in the absence of such a law, is not morally prohibited, such as being married to two or more people simultaneously. It can also require behavior that, without such a law, is not morally required, such as giving money to the government. With regard to morally controversial matters, about which equally informed rational persons disagree, such as abortion, the law can either prohibit or allow it. Equally informed rational persons disagree about whether fetuses are included in the group that is impartially protected by morality, partially protected, or not protected at all. The law can allow behavior that some people regard as morally unacceptable, such as early abortion, and it can prohibit behavior that some people regard as morally acceptable, such as late abortion. No one thinks that what the law decides about abortion settles the moral issue. However, except for fanatics, everyone holds that when an issue is morally unresolvable, the law can provide practical guidance, although there may be some asymmetry in this attitude. There is general agreement that if the law permits some behavior that is morally controversial—for example, abortion—then no one should inflict harms on people, or threaten to, in order to prevent them from behaving in the permitted way. However, if the law prohibits that same behavior, then civil disobedience would be weakly justified if the law results in some moral agents suffering significant harm, and a significant number of moral agents regard their avoiding that harm as an adequate justification for violating the law.

It is absolutely clear that the fetus should be impartially protected from harm by anyone other than the pregnant woman. If the woman does not want her fetus killed, then it is immoral to kill it. To kill it is to harm the woman who does not want her fetus to be killed. However, if it is the pregnant woman herself who wants the fetus aborted, then, with the possible exception of the expectant father, no moral agent is being harmed when the fetus is aborted. When dealing with a controversial moral issue, a person is not harmed if someone else acts contrary to the way in which he thinks people morally ought to act. On the contrary, in morally controversial matters, morality prohibits private individuals from depriving people of the freedom to act as the law permits, unless they have an objectively adequate reason for doing so.

::

The Role of Governments in Settling Unresolvable Moral Disagreements

Although disagreement about the facts, especially disagreement about the probabilities of the good and bad consequences of various alternatives, is the greatest source of moral disagreement, everyone agrees that this kind of disagreement does not pose any theoretical problems. What many philosophers deny is that equally informed, impartial rational persons can disagree about what morally ought to be done. Actually, these philosophers do not deny that there are four sources of moral disagreement among equally informed, impartial rational persons; rather, they simply ignore these sources. Careful examination of serious moral discussion makes it clear that equally informed, impartial rational persons disagree about (1) the scope of morality, such as whether fetuses are impartially protected, or protected at all, by morality; (2) the rankings of the various goods and evils, such as whether a specified loss of freedom is worse than a specified risk of death; (3) the harmful and beneficial consequences of a violation being publicly allowed and of it not being publicly allowed, when these are based on ideological views that are not open to empirical investigation; and (4) the interpretation of a moral rule, such as whether turning off the respirator of a ventilator-dependent patient who has refused further treatment counts as killing him. (But this disagreement is partially based on one or more of the previous sources of disagreement.)

These disagreements are responsible for all of the morally unresolvable questions. Some persons have such strong views about how people ought to behave in these morally controversial situations that they do not recognize that it is morally acceptable to have a different view. As Hobbes pointed out, it is moral and religious disagreement rather than self-interest that creates the need for a government strong enough to enforce obedience to its decisions about how its citizens should behave in these morally controversial situations. One of the proper functions of governments is to provide a legal or political solution to those morally unresolvable questions that need to be settled.

It is a function of government, either by legislation or by judicial decision, to determine who besides moral agents is in the group impartially protected, or protected at all, by morality. Governments can declare that a fetus belongs in the group that is impartially protected by morality only after its head has emerged from the woman's body. They can also declare that fetuses are in the group impartially protected from the time of conception, implantation, or viability, or they can pick a time, such as six months after conception. They can also declare that fetuses are not protected at all at one of these times, partially protected at a later time, and impartially protected at a still later time. Or they can declare that fetuses are not protected at all at any time. They can even declare that neonates are not impartially protected, or even protected at all, although unless the neonate will never become a moral agent, few governments are likely to do this. Governments can also declare that some animals are partially protected and can even declare that some are impartially protected. However, unless they were decisively influenced by religious considerations, it would be almost impossible to imagine why they would do the latter. But many governments have laws preventing cruelty to animals. Even those who regard animals as not protected at all by morality are morally required to obey those laws.

Governments also decide on the ranking of some goods and evils; most hold that the freedom to go seventy-five miles an hour is not worth the additional risk of injury and death that would result. Speed limits are the clearest examples of a government ranking such goods and evils, but many health requirements, such as vaccinations, building codes, and so on, are also examples of the government deciding that the harms to be avoided justify the relevant deprivation of freedom. These government decisions need not be based solely on the rankings of the goods and evils; they may also be based on government estimates of the harmful and beneficial consequences of depriving their citizens of some specific freedom. In particular cases, courts may decide whether a violation of a moral rule is justified by the harm that is avoided or prevented, such as deciding that in the circumstances it is justified for a person not to abide by his contract. Although individuals may disagree with a court's or legislators' ranking of the goods and evils or with their estimates of the harmful and beneficial consequences, as long as the rankings and estimates are rational, citizens are morally required to obey the law. Only when all informed impartial rational persons would publicly allow violating the law is it strongly justified to violate a law. Although morality is above the law, individual consciences are not.

Governments also decide how a moral rule is to be interpreted in their countries. They decide whether an advertisement is deceptive, and different governments may make different decisions. They also decide whether some contracts violate the rule against deceiving. Everyone agrees that a court decides whether a killing is justified, such as deciding whether it was done in self-defense or in the lawful performance of a duty. Everyone also agrees that a court can decide whether a killing was excusable, such as deciding that there was no way for the agent to know that his act would result in someone's death. But justified or excused killing is still killing, and governments can also decide whether some act that results in someone's death even counts as killing. A government can decide that a physician who, on the basis of a valid refusal of continuing treatment by a ventilator-dependent patient, turns off the ventilator has not killed the patient but only allowed the patient to die.

Rights

Everyone has the right not to be killed, not to be caused pain, not to be disabled, and not to be deprived of freedom or pleasure. These are not merely legal rights but are basic human or moral rights. It is not an accident that these basic rights correspond to the first five moral rules. To have a right not to be killed is just to have the protection of a moral rule prohibiting killing. The close relationship between moral rules and rights can be seen from the fact that only moral agents can break moral rules or violate rights.[30] Nothing a dog does counts either as breaking a moral rule or as violating a person's rights. To have one of these basic rights is simply to have the protection of the corresponding moral rule. If a person validly consents to having his doctor cause him pain, as patients generally do when they consent to an operation, then his right not to be caused pain has not been violated. To have a basic right violated is to have a moral rule broken with regard to a person without her valid consent.

Moral agents also have the right not to be deceived, not to have promises broken, and not to be cheated. These are also basic rights and to violate them is to break the corresponding rule with regard to a person without her valid consent. It is less clear whether people have the right not to have duties toward them neglected or the right not to have laws affecting them broken. The moral rules concerning duties and laws seem not to be essentially related to individuals and so do not seem to yield rights in the same way that the first eight moral rules do. However, whenever a violation of either of these two moral rules results in a person being killed, caused pain, disabled, deprived of freedom or pleasure, deceived, having a promise broken, or cheated, then he has had his rights violated. Just as there can be justified violations of moral rules even without the valid consent of the person toward whom the rule is being violated, so there can be justified violations of a person's rights. Whatever justifies the violation of a moral rule justifies the corresponding violation of a person's right. The same facts are morally relevant, the same two-step procedure should be used, and the same three outcomes—unjustified, weakly justified, and strongly justified—are possible.

This close correspondence between rights and moral rules may make it seem as if rights, although they are powerful rhetorically, are theoretically dispensable. This may be true of the basic rights mentioned above, but it is not true of those rights, like the right to privacy, that seem to be of more interest to people. Rights like the right to privacy are interpretations of the moral rules. If one person looks at or listens to another person and that person is upset by being looked at or listened to, then the question arises whether the first person caused the second person to be upset. This question is not about causality in any scientific sense; it is a question about whether the first person should be regarded as violating the moral rule prohibiting causing pain with regard to the second. Suppose the second person is a celebrity and is in a public place and the first person is a reporter/photographer trying to write a story about him and is following him wherever he goes. Should the celebrity's feeling of annoyance be regarded as being caused by the reporter/photographer, or should it be regarded as being the celebrity's own fault?

If the court decides that the reporter/photographer should be held responsible for the annoyance of the celebrity, they could state that conclusion by stating that the celebrity's right to privacy has been violated. They would have interpreted the rule prohibiting causing pain in such a way that a person's becoming annoyed at being followed around, looked at, and listened to all day is regarded as a violation of that moral rule. This violation of a person's right to privacy is a violation of an interpretation of the rule prohibiting causing pain. Negative rights, except for the basic rights, correspond to interpretations of the basic moral rules. Societies differ from one another in their interpretations of moral rules, so the scope of the right to privacy and even whether there is any right of privacy can differ in different societies. Even within a single society interpretations can change, so that the right of privacy can expand or contract. That, within limits, societies can differ in their interpretations of moral rules is the small grain of truth in the position of ethical relativism.

Positive rights are distinct from the negative rights discussed above. All positive rights, like the right to health care or the right to education, are equivalent to duties on the part of governments. If a person has a right to health care, then her government has a duty to provide health care. The basic negative rights are moral rights; they are simply having the protection of the moral rules. The negative rights that are interpretations of moral rules are primarily moral rights, but because governments may interpret the rules, these rights may be partly political as well. Positive rights are completely political rights. They are addressed to governments and they claim that these governments have duties to provide health care and education. The level of health care and education has to be dependent on the resources of the government and the demands on those resources. The most plausible way of determining the level of health care and education that people have a right to is by using the same concept of an impartial rational person that is used in the moral theory. A person has a right to a level of health care such that all impartial rational persons, knowing the resources of a society and the demands on those resources, would favor all members of that society having at least that level of health care. They would regard any person in that society with less than that level of health care as deprived.

⁇
The Consequences of Morality Not Always Providing a Unique Correct Answer

If a person accepts the standard view of moral theories that morality always provides a unique correct answer to every moral question about how one morally ought to act, then all moral disagreements must be explained away. Those who disagree must be not equally informed, not impartial, or not rational. If two people who hold the standard view are discussing a controversial moral issue and disagree with each other, they must regard the other as ignorant, partial, or irrational. These are not the attitudes that make for a respectful and fruitful discussion of a controversial moral issue. However, if both hold the view that morality does not always provide unique correct answers to moral questions, then they may conclude, usually correctly, that this is one of these issues. Then they need not regard the other person's view as morally unacceptable and can cooperate in trying to find out the source of their disagreement.

It is usually clear if the disagreement is about the scope of morality. Most disagreements about abortion and the treatment of animals have their source in that kind of disagreement, and almost no other moral disagreements have that as their source. Most other moral disagreements have as their ultimate source a difference in the rankings of the goods and evils or a difference in the estimates of the harmful and beneficial consequences of everyone knowing that a certain kind of violation is allowed. Although there can be differing interpretations of the moral rules, these differing interpretations are usually based on differences in the rankings or the estimates. An impartial rational person will interpret a moral rule in a way that she regards as resulting in the least amount of overall harm. Deciding what interpretation of a moral rule to adopt is completely parallel to the second step of the two-step procedure to be used when deciding what violation of a moral rule is justified. Which interpretation is adopted should be determined by comparing the estimate of the consequences of everyone knowing that the rule is interpreted in one way with the estimate of the consequences of everyone knowing that the rule is interpreted in some other way.

Often there will be differences in the estimates or of the ranking of those consequences by different people or by different societies.

People who have served on hospital ethics committees or on similar ethical decision-making bodies know how liberating it is to realize that on the most controversial questions, no one need be putting forward a wrong answer. This realization allows a person to compromise without losing her moral integrity. It allows people to work together to find a solution that, while it may not completely satisfy anyone, satisfies everyone to some degree. It allows those in a subordinate decision-making capacity to accept the decision of the person who has the final authority for making a decision while at the same time allowing the person with the final authority to acknowledge the acceptability of alternative views. It allows people to try to persuade each other, without implying that the other person is wrong.

These features are of great importance in political theory. To hold the standard view that there is a unique correct answer to every moral question does not naturally incline one to support a democratic form of government. Unless a person holds that there are insuperable epistemological obstacles to finding out the correct answer, the natural result of holding the standard view is to favor a government composed of those who are most likely to know the correct answers to moral questions. However, if, on the issues about which there are likely to be disagreements, there are often no unique correct answers, then it is most natural for a person to endorse reaching a decision that is favored by the most people. Only a theory that allows that there is often no unique correct answer, especially on controversial matters, provides a moral argument for deciding the issue democratically. Of course, a morally acceptable democracy must not make any decisions that no impartial rational person could support, but within these limits, a democracy seems the best way to reach a decision when there is no best moral decision. A moral theory that does not provide a decision procedure that settles every moral problem allows for unresolvable moral disagreement. Such a theory might seem to be inferior to one that does provide such a decision procedure. However, more careful examination of both kinds of theories shows that the opposite is in fact true.

A Complete Moral Theory

A complete moral theory should not be taken to be a theory that provides a unique answer to every moral question. Rather, a complete moral theory should explain and justify the overwhelming agreement on most moral matters while at the same time explaining and justifying the limited disagreement on some of the most important moral matters. Moral theories that provide no explanation or justification for unresolvable moral disagreement are incomplete; those that claim there are no unresolvable moral disagreements are false.

A complete moral theory must not only provide analyses of the three concepts that are central to any account of morality—that of morality itself, of impartiality, and of rationality—but also show how these concepts are related to each other. A complete theory must also relate morality to human nature, making it clear why any beings having the essential features of human nature such as fallibility, rationality, and vulnerability would develop a system of morality with all of the features of our common morality. Although common morality is a system, it does not remove the need for human judgment. It is true that common morality is systematic enough that a computer could be programmed so that, provided with the facts of the case, it always comes up with acceptable moral answers. However, another computer could be programmed differently and still always come up with acceptable answers. There is no computer program that can tell you which of the competing computer programs you should adopt.

⠓
Conclusion

We often hear the complaint that scientific advances are outstripping moral advances, as if we need to make new moral discoveries to deal with the new scientific discoveries and technology. We do need to understand how common morality applies to new situations, but there is no need for moral advances. Common morality, together with an understanding of the new situations created by scientific discoveries and technology, is sufficient to deal with any problem with which we are confronted. However, many people would prefer to make morality seem problematic. It is much harder to act immorally if you recognize that what you are doing is clearly immoral. Hobbes claims that if our interests were as affected by geometry as much as they are by morality, we would have no more agreement in geometry than we have in morality.[31] The purpose of this book is to provide such a clear, coherent, and comprehensive description of morality and its justification, so that no one will be able to deceive himself or others about the moral acceptability of his actions. This will not eliminate immoral behavior, but by making it harder to defend immoral policies, it may contribute to the goal of common morality, which is the lessening of the amount of harm suffered.

Rationality Flow Chart
Is your action (objectively) irrational?*

Will your action cause, or significantly increase the probability of, you or anyone for whom you care suffering some nontrivial harm?

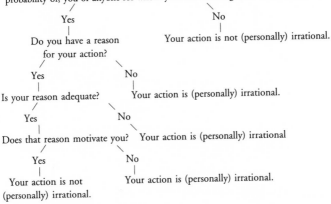

Yes

Is there a reason for your action?

No — Your action is not (objectively) irrational.

Yes

Is that reason adequate?

No — Your action is (objectively) irrational.

Yes — Your action is not (objectively) irrational.

No — Your action is (objectively) irrational.

Is your action (personally) irrational?

Do you, or should you, believe that your action will cause, or significantly increase the probability of, you or anyone for whom you care suffering some nontrivial harm?

Yes

Do you have a reason for your action?

No — Your action is not (personally) irrational.

Yes

Is your reason adequate?

No — Your action is (personally) irrational.

Yes

Does that reason motivate you? — Your action is (personally) irrational

No — Your action is (personally) irrational.

Yes — Your action is not (personally) irrational.

People can disagree about the adequacy of a reason, but if any significant group of otherwise rational people regard a reason as adequate, the reason does count as adequate.

*These flow charts were suggested by and derived from Heather Gert.

Morality Flow Chart
Is your action immoral?*

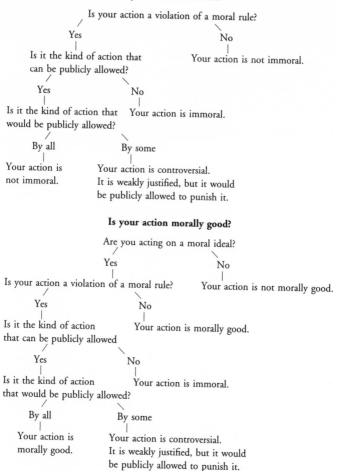

Is your action a violation of a moral rule?

Yes   No

Is it the kind of action that   Your action is not immoral.
can be publicly allowed?

Yes   No

Is it the kind of action that   Your action is immoral.
would be publicly allowed?

By all   By some

Your action is   Your action is controversial.
not immoral.   It is weakly justified, but it would
be publicly allowed to punish it.

Is your action morally good?

Are you acting on a moral ideal?

Yes   No

Is your action a violation of a moral rule?   Your action is not morally good.

Yes   No

Is it the kind of action   Your action is morally good.
that can be publicly allowed

Yes   No

Is it the kind of action   Your action is immoral.
that would be publicly allowed?

By all   By some

Your action is   Your action is controversial.
morally good.   It is weakly justified, but it would
be publicly allowed to punish it.

An action can be publicly allowed only if it would be rational for a person using only rationally required beliefs to favor everyone knowing that this kind of action is allowed.

---

*These flow charts were suggested by and derived from Heather Gert.

⠸ Glossary for Common Morality

Arrogance: not accepting that one is subject to the same moral system that applies to all other moral agents; not accepting that one shares all of the morally significant characteristics of all moral agents, including limited knowledge, fallibility, and vulnerability; violating a moral rule when one would not be willing for everyone to know that they may violate the rule in the same circumstances; using beliefs that one knows are not shared by all moral agents to determine what kinds of actions the moral system prohibits, requires, discourages, or encourages: incompatible with moral impartiality.

Blindfold of Justice: requires using only those beliefs that are rationally required, i.e., those that all moral agents have, to determine what kinds of actions the moral system prohibits, requires, discourages, or encourages; however it does not require ranking the different evils (harms) and goods (benefits) in the same way as other moral agents.

Common morality: see morality.

Evil (harm): that which all rational persons avoid unless they have an adequate reason not to; basic evils are death, pain, disability, loss of freedom, and loss of pleasure.

Good (benefit): that which no rational person avoids without an adequate reason: basic goods are abilities, consciousness, freedom, and pleasure; it might be useful to add resources and security to this list, but this would not require any addition to the list of evils, as depriving of resources or security clearly counts as causing a loss of freedom.

Humility: accepting that morality applies to one in the same way that it applies to all other moral agents; accepting that one shares all of the morally significant characteristics of all moral agents, including limited knowledge, fallibility, and vulnerability.

Impartiality: the standard kind of impartiality applies when one is not a member of the group toward which impartiality is required, e.g., umpires and judges. It cannot be understood unless specified with respect to the kind of action and with regard to the group toward which one is impartial in this respect; persons act impartially in respect R with regard to group G if and only if their actions in respect R are not influenced by which member(s) of group G benefit or are harmed by their actions.

Impartiality, moral: this not only includes the standard kind of impartiality with respect to obeying or violating a moral rule with regard to at least all moral agents but also includes not violating a moral rule, unless one would be willing for everyone to know that they can violate the rule in the same morally relevant circumstances.

Irrational action, objective: an action that will result in harm to the agent or to someone for whom the agent cares when there is not an adequate reason for the action.

Irrational action, personal: an action that an agent believes or should believe will result in harm to her/him or to someone for whom the agent cares without having a rational belief that there is an adequate reason for the action.

Irrational belief: belief that it would be irrational for this moral agent, given her/his intelligence and knowledge, to have; rationally prohibited belief, i.e., belief that it would be irrational for any moral agent to have.

Moral agent: a rational person who knows and understands what kinds of actions morality prohibits, requires, discourages, encourages, and allows, and who has the ability to guide her/his behavior accordingly; someone who is morally responsible for her/his behavior.

Moral attitude: the attitude toward the moral rules that all impartial moral agents would take; that they be obeyed unless an impartial moral agent can publicly allow violating the rule in circumstances with the same morally relevant features. But unless all impartial moral agents would publicly allow the violation, the moral attitude does not encourage that it should be violated in these circumstances.

Moral decision: a decision by a moral agent to do or refrain from doing an action to which the moral system applies.

Moral disagreement: disagreement among impartial moral agents about the moral decision or moral judgment that should be made. The most common source of moral disagreement is disagreement about the facts, but there can be other sources.

Moral disagreement, unresolvable: the four sources of unresolvable moral disagreement are differences about (1) the scope of morality (who is protected by the moral system, and how much); (2) the rankings of the evils (harms) and good (benefits); (3) ideology; unverifiable estimates of the beneficial and harmful consequences of everyone knowing that a particular kind of violation of a moral rule is allowed and is not allowed; (4) interpretations of moral rules.

Moral ideal: that part of the moral system that encourages acting in order to lessen the suffering of harm by anyone protected by the moral system, e.g., aid the needy and relieve pain.

Moral judgment: a judgment by a moral agent about the actions, character, or motives of a moral agent, made on the basis of the moral system.

Moral rule: that part of the moral system the violation of which is morally prohibited unless an impartial moral agent could favor everyone knowing that the rule may be violated in the same circumstances, that is, circumstances with the same morally relevant features, e.g., "do not kill" and "do not deceive."

Moral system: see morality; an informal public system that applies to all those who know and understand it and can guide their behavior accordingly.

Moral theory: An explicit description of the moral system together with its justification. This requires accounts of the concepts of morality, of impartiality, of rationality, and of their interrelationships.

Moral worth: a measure of what an action shows about the moral character of the person performing it.

Morality: an informal public system applying to all moral agents, that is, rational persons with sufficient knowledge and intelligence to understand it and the voluntary abilities to guide their behavior by it, governing behavior that affects others, and including what are commonly known as the moral rules, ideals, and virtues and that has the lessening of evil (harm) suffered by those protected by the system as its goal.

Morally allowed, or what morality allows: not morally prohibited, required, discouraged, or encouraged; ambiguous, as it can mean either that impartial moral agents agree that is covered by the moral system but disagree whether it belongs in any of the four categories mentioned above, or that they agree that it is not covered by the moral system at all.

Morally bad action: an action that the moral system discourages moral agents from performing; all impartial moral agents would discourage such actions.

Morally good action: an action that the moral system encourages moral agents to perform; all impartial moral agents would encourage such actions.

Morally indifferent action: an action to which the moral system does not apply.

Morally relevant feature: a feature of an action that must be used in providing a description of the kind of violation of a moral rule under consideration, e.g., the relationship between the violator and the person toward whom the rule is violated, whether there are alternative actions that would be preferable. Describing an act in terms of its morally relevant features is the first step of the two-step procedure used in deciding whether to publicly allow that kind of violation.

Morally right action: an action that the moral system requires moral agents to perform; all impartial moral agents would require such action.

Morally wrong action: an action that the moral system prohibits moral agents from performing; all impartial moral agents would prohibit such actions.

Motive: a belief that the agent takes as explaining why he acted as he did and which is part of the explanation for his acting in that way; need not be a reason.

Public system: a system that has the following two features: (1) All persons whose behavior is to be guided and judged by that system understand it, and know what kind of behavior the system prohibits, requires, discourages, encourages, and allows. (2) It is not irrational for any of these persons to accept being guided and judged by that system.

Public system, informal: a public system that does not have a decision procedure that resolves all disputes.

Publicly allow: be willing for everyone to know that this kind of moral rule violation is allowed.

Punishment: infliction of an evil (harm) by an authorized person for a violation of a moral rule.

Rational: not irrational.

Rational belief: a belief that is not irrational.

Rational persons: persons insofar as their actions, beliefs, and desires are rational.

Rationally allowed action: an action that is not irrational to do and not irrational not to do.

Rationally allowed belief: a belief that is neither rationally prohibited nor rationally required.

Rationally allowed desire: a desire that is neither rationally prohibited nor rationally required.

Rationally prohibited action: an action that it would be irrational for any moral agent to do.

Rationally prohibited belief: a belief that it would be irrational for any moral agent to have, e.g., I am invulnerable, I am infallible, no one knows anything about the world outside of their own minds.

Rationally prohibited desire: a desire for an evil (harm) or to avoid a good (benefit) without an adequate reason; a desire to do an irrational action.

Rationally required action: an action that it would be irrational for any moral agent not to do.

Rationally required belief: a belief that it would be irrational for any moral agent not to have, e.g., no moral agent is invulnerable; no moral agent is infallible.

Rationally required desire: a desire to avoid an evil (harm); a desire to avoid doing an irrational action.

Reason: a rational belief or fact of a kind that can make some otherwise irrational action rational, although it may not make the particular action for which it is a reason rational; basic reasons concern avoiding, preventing, or relieving (evils) harms, or gaining goods (benefits).

Reason, adequate: a rational belief or fact that can make the otherwise irrational action for which it is a reason rational.

Reason, best: an ambiguous phrase; it can mean either a reason with the greatest justifying force or a reason with the greatest requiring force.

Reason, better: an ambiguous phrase; it can mean either a reason with more justifying force than another reason or a reason with more requiring force than another reason.

Reason, justifying force of: one reason has more justifying force than another if it can make rational every otherwise irrational act that the other reason can, plus others besides; the justifying force of a reason depends solely on the amount of harm avoided, prevented, or relieved, or the amount of good gained, without reference to who is benefited; all reasons have justifying force.

Reason, objective: a fact that one's action will result in less evil (harm) or more good (benefit) for someone.

Reason, personal: a rational belief that one's action will result in less evil (harm) or more good (benefit) for someone.

Reason, requiring force of: one reason has more requiring force than another if failing to act on it can make irrational every act that failing to act on the other reason can, plus others besides. Only reasons related to avoiding, preventing, or relieving harm to the agent directly or indirectly have requiring force, thus a reason can have a high justifying force and a high requiring force, or a high justifying force but no requiring force.

Two-step procedure: procedure for determining if a violation of a moral rule is strongly justified, weakly justified, or unjustified. The first step involves describing the act using only its morally relevant features. The second step involves estimating the good and bad consequences of everyone knowing that this kind of violation is allowed and estimating the good and bad consequences of everyone knowing that this kind of violation is not allowed, and comparing these estimates.

Vice, moral: a trait of character that involves either more unjustified violations of moral rules or less justified following of moral ideals than would be performed by most people in the same situations: a trait of character that all impartial moral agents want no one to have, e.g., cruelty and callousness.

Vice, personal: a trait of character that involves acting irrationally when confronted with e.g., danger, temptation, and strong emotions: a trait of character that no rational person wants for herself, e.g., cowardice, imprudence, and intemperance.

Violation, same kind of: a violation in the same circumstances, i.e., with the same morally relevant features.

Violation, strongly justified: a violation that all impartial moral agents would publicly allow.

Violation, unjustified: a violation that no impartial moral agent would publicly allow.

Violation, weakly justified: a violation that some impartial moral agents would publicly allow and that some impartial moral agents would not publicly allow.

Virtue, moral: a trait of character that involves either fewer unjustified violations of moral rules or more justified following of moral ideals than would be performed by most people in the same situations; a trait of character that all impartial moral agents want everyone to have, e.g., fairness, truthfulness, and kindness.

Virtue, personal: a trait of character that involves acting rationally even when confronted with e.g., danger, temptation, or strong emotions: a trait of character that all rational persons want for themselves, e.g., courage, prudence, and temperance.

Virtue, social: a trait of character that promotes harmonious social interaction among persons, e.g., friendliness, generosity, and gratefulness.

Volitional ability: ability to will to do and to will not to do a kind of action.

Voluntary ability: ability to do and not to do a kind of voluntary action; requires having the relevant mental ability, physical ability, and volitional ability.

Voluntary action: an intentional action of a kind that one has the ability to will to do and to will not to do.

Will to do: intentionally do or try to do.

⁑ Notes

Preface

1. See "Morality versus Slogans," *Western Michigan University Center for the Study of Ethics in Society* 3, no. 2 (December 1989).
2. I mention these two philosophers only to make explicit, to those who know about them, some views that I do not accept. I also do not accept social-contract theories, such as John Rawls's *A Theory of Justice.* However, it is not necessary to know any of these views in order to understand my description of morality and its justification.

Introduction

1. Whenever I talk about rational persons I mean persons insofar as they are rational.
2. This is the great insight of all natural-law theories of morality. The failure to recognize that this is an essential feature of morality is responsible for the inadequacy of all the standard consequentialist accounts of morality, including all rule consequentialists, who claim that which rules are the correct moral rules must be determined by empirical investigation.
3. When I talk about moral agents, I mean those rational persons who understand what morality prohibits, requires, etc., can act on their understanding, and, hence, except in special circumstances, are fully responsible for their actions. It is possible for children and people who are mildly retarded to be partial moral agents because they may understand some of the prohibitions and requirements of morality, but not all of them.

4. From now on, whenever I talk about all moral agents agreeing or disagreeing on some moral matter, I mean moral agents who use only those beliefs about the world that are accepted by all moral agents. If, for example, religious beliefs were used, there might not be agreement among moral agents about anything. The further reasons for this limitation will be discussed in part II.

5. For a fuller account of morality, see "The Definition of Morality" in the *Stanford Online Encyclopedia of Philosophy* (plato.stanford.edu/entries/**morality**-definition/).

Part I: The Moral System

1. This may make it seem as if my account of morality is a form of consequentialism, but this is true only if consequentialism is taken as including any view that takes consequences to be important, rather than as a view that says only consequences matter. This point will be discussed in more detail in part II.

2. Many people use the phrase "morally wrong" to characterize any action or decision that they would prohibit any moral agent from doing. This is not an incorrect use of "morally wrong," but I prefer to restrict the application of "morally wrong" to those actions or decisions that all moral agents would prohibit any moral agent from doing. Confusion between these two uses of "morally wrong" may mislead some people into thinking that all fully informed moral agents would agree with their moral judgment on a controversial matter when that is not true. I claim only that the moral system will yield all first-order moral judgments, for example, "Except under extreme circumstances no one morally ought to have an abortion." I do not claim that it will yield all second-order moral judgments, for example, "His moral judgment that abortion is always morally acceptable is mistaken."

3. In languages other than English there may be different formulations that would be more easily understood.

4. Kant also recognizes the greater importance of the moral rules. "If such a way of thinking [not helping others] were to become a universal law of nature, the human race admittedly could very well subsist and doubtless could subsist even better than when everyone prates about

sympathy and benevolence and even on occasion exerts himself to practice them but, on the other hand, also cheats when he can, betrays the rights of man, or otherwise violates them" (*Grounding for the Metaphysics of Morals* [1785] translated by James Wellingon (Indianapolis, IN: Hackett Publishing Company, 1981), p. 32, AK 423).

5. This example was originally proposed by Dan Brock in his contribution to the *Philosophy and Phenomenological Research* symposium on my book *Morality: Its Nature and Justification* (*Philosophy and Phenomenological Research* 62, no. 2 [March 2001]): 435–440.

6. Violating the moral rules with regard to former agents who are still conscious must also be justified, because moral agents know that they can cease to be moral agents and still be conscious and so still be able to suffer harm.

7. All moral agents are aware that many moral agents are as concerned with infants and children as they are with any moral agents, including themselves. This is sufficient to explain why infants and children are almost universally regarded as being impartially protected.

8. Even now, and even more commonly in the past, women and those of a different race are sometimes not regarded as having the full protection of the moral rules. There is now near universal recognition that this is a mistake, that a person's gender or race is irrelevant to being a moral agent. Since fetuses and nonhuman animals are, in fact, not moral agents, there is no reason to believe that there will ever be the same level of agreement about extending the impartial protection of the moral rules to them.

9. I have adopted this spelling to distinguish Wittgenstein's use of "criteria" from the normal senses of "criterion" and "criteria." For a fuller explanation, see my "Criterian and Human Nature," in *Wittgenstein: Eine Neubewertung; Toward a Reevaluation,* edited by Rudolf Haller and Johannes Brandl (Vein: Verlag Hölder-Pichler-Tempsky, 1990), vol. 2, 106–14.

10. See Charles Darwin, *The Expression of the Emotions in Man and Animals* [1872], 3d ed. (Oxford: Oxford University Press, 1998).

11. All of the unpleasant emotions (e.g., envy, grief, and shame) involve one or more of these feelings.

12. The proper method for interpreting a moral rule is similar to the second step of the two-step procedure for deciding whether a violation of a moral rule is justified.

13. See Heather J. Gert, "Rights and Rights Violators: A New Approach to the Nature of Rights," *Journal of Philosophy* 87, no. 12 (December 1990): 688–94.

14. For a fuller account of volitional abilities and disabilities and of intentional, voluntary, and free actions, see Bernard Gert and Timothy Duggan, "Free Will as the Ability to Will," *Nous* 13, no. 2 (1979): 197–217; reprinted in *Moral Responsibility*, edited by John Martin Fisher (Ithaca, NY: Cornell University Press, 1986).

15. See J. L. Austin, "Performative Utterances," in *Philosophical Papers* (Oxford: Oxford University Press, 1961), 220–40. "I promise" is the paradigm case of a performative utterance. It sounds as if I am merely describing what I am doing (namely, promising), but in the appropriate circumstances, saying "I promise" is promising. Hobbes made this same point in his discussion of the giving up of a right. See *Leviathan*, chap. 14, pars. 7–16.

16. One also has a duty if one is a member of a small group, and the small group meets the three conditions mentioned, e.g., a small brush fire that will cause great harm if not put out now when it would be easy to do so.

17. Duties of imperfect obligation are actions covered by a moral ideal.

18. Duties of perfect obligation are actions covered by a moral rule.

19. The view that moral rules should never be broken is a strict deontology. The view that breaking a moral rule needs a justification stronger than simply that the consequences of breaking the rule will be better than the consequences of keeping it is a moderate deontology. Common morality has many similarities to this kind of moderate deontology, differing from other deontological views in requiring that the moral system, including all of the moral rules, be known to all moral agents.

20. This view, which can be taken as one form of a view called rule consequentialism, seems to result in moral decisions and judgments that are identical to act consequentialism. Another form of rule

consequentialism is the view that genuine moral rules are those that never have better consequences when broken. On this view, which is not Mill's, it is impossible for anyone to know the moral rules or for them ever to be stated. Some forms of rule consequentialism hold that, although moral rules sometimes are justifiably broken, the fact that the total consequences, both direct and indirect, of the particular act of breaking a rule are better does not by itself justify breaking the rule. This form of rule consequentialism is a kind of moderate deontology and has many similarities to common morality, but common morality differs from all standard forms of rule consequentialism in requiring that the moral system, including all of the moral rules, be known to all moral agents.

21. The formulation of the Categorical Imperative that I am concerned with is "Act only on that maxim that you can thereby will to be a universal law of nature." It is often taken as characterizing the kind of impartiality required by morality.

22. This is due to the lottery nature of punishment. Although unforeseeable consequences do not justify inflicting greater punishment than is authorized by the law, the law can take into account the actual, although unforeseeable, consequences of the violation in setting the punishment.

23. Morally relevant feature 3 should also explicitly include whether the (implied or explicit) ranking of the harms and goods is rational or irrational. This is important because only when the implied ranking is irrational is the difference between the harms caused and the harms prevented great enough to justify acting paternalistically.

24. See *Leviathan*, chap. 15, par. 19, the seventh natural law. See also *De Cive*, chap. 3, sec. 11, the sixth natural law.

25. See J. L. Bernat, B. Gert, and R. P. Mogielnicki, "Patient Refusal of Hydration and Nutrition: An Alternative to Physician Assisted Suicide or Voluntary Euthanasia," *Archives of Internal Medicine* 153 (December 27, 1993): 2723–28; and Bernard Gert, Charles M. Culver, and K. Danner Clouser, *Bioethics: A Systematic Approach* (Oxford: Oxford University Press, 2006), 323–338.

26. See note 20.

27. The Doctrine of Double Effect is incorrect in claiming that it is always wrong to intentionally violate a moral rule or cause harm even when this is necessary in order to prevent much more serious harm.

28. See Bernard Gert, Charles M. Culver, and K. Danner Clouser, *Bioethics: A Systematic Approach* (Oxford: Oxford University Press, 2006), chap. 10, for a discussion of examples of medical paternalism involving deception.

29. For an example using the moral system to reason about whether it is morally acceptable to illegally copy software, see my article "Common Morality and Computers," *Ethics and Information Technology* 1, no. 1 (1999): 57–64. For further development of reasoning about this case, see Timm Triplett's review article "Bernard Gert's *Morality* and Its Application to Computer Ethics," *Ethics and Information Technology* 4, no. 1 (2002): 70–92.

Part II. The Moral Theory

1. Because I am concerned only with rational persons who have all of the characteristics necessary to be a moral agent, I shall use "moral agent" and "rational person" to refer to the same person. Which phrase I use, "rational person" or "moral agent," will be determined by which feature seems more relevant in the context, but it should be possible to switch phrases without any change in the truth of what I say. Also, as I said in note 1 of the Introduction, whenever I talk about rational persons (or moral agents) I mean persons insofar as they are rational.

2. When I talk about people for whom a person is concerned, I am referring to people for whom that person cares as much or more than anyone else affected, including herself.

3. Unless there is a restriction to rationally required beliefs or to beliefs that are regarded by all qualified persons as true, it is impossible to prove or justify any conclusions. Descartes believed that God could make $2 + 2 = 5$. If this kind of belief is not ruled out, then there cannot even be any mathematical proofs. Usually this restriction remains implicit. It is necessary to make it explicit in this situation because the restriction to rationally required beliefs rules out some true beliefs. Except for beliefs that all moral agents have about themselves, no

personal beliefs can be used. This means that a person cannot use any beliefs about her age, ethnic group, gender, intelligence, nationality, physical status, race, or religion, even though she is as justifiably confident that these beliefs are true as she is that the rationally required beliefs are true.

4. This is equivalent to seeking agreement among all rational persons. Following a suggestion by Ernst Tugendhat, this point could also be put as follows: she wants to justify to the other persons the adoption of common morality as the public system to govern the behavior of all moral agents, but she knows only that the other persons also are moral agents who have all of the rationally required beliefs and desires.

5. Rational persons know that rational persons have different rankings of the goods and evils. A person's decisions will be affected by his rankings even if he is not aware of those rankings. If it is appropriate to talk about a person knowing his own rankings, then this is the only kind of idiosyncratic personal knowledge that people can have about themselves.

6. Seeking agreement with persons about whom one knows only that they have all of the rationally required beliefs and desires is functionally equivalent to seeking agreement among all rational persons.

7. See note 14, part I.

8. John Rawls, *A Theory of Justice* (Cambridge: Harvard University Press, 1971).

9. Technically, there is no contradiction if there are no rational persons who are impartial with respect to the moral rules with regard to all moral agents. Paul McNamara pointed out the need for this addition to the argument.

10. I realize that, semantically, "irrational" means "not rational" and so it seems obvious that one has to know what counts as acting rationally before one can know what counts as acting irrationally. However, when "rational" and "irrational" are taken as the fundamental normative concepts, the previous discussion shows that this is not true. Mill makes a similar point when claiming that "justice, like many other moral attributes, is best defined by its opposite" (*Utilitarianism,* chap. 5, par. 3). J. L. Austin makes a similar point about negative

terms being more basic than positive terms (e.g., "real") in *Sense and Sensibilia* (Oxford: Clarendon Press, 1962), 70, and more generally in "A Plea for Excuses," in *Philosophical Papers* (Oxford: Oxford University Press, 1961), 140.

11. For an account of mental disorders see the *Diagnostic and Statistical Manual of Mental Disorders, DSM-IV-TR* (American Psychiatric Association, 2000).

12. Richard Brandt's account of a rational action in *A Theory of the Right and the Good* (Oxford University Press, 1979) has this result.

13. Doing an action that is called for by a rule the general following of which avoids or prevents harmful consequences counts as acting to significantly decrease the probability of these consequences. It is a reason for doing an action that it is called for by such a rule.

14. What counts as a significant number is a matter of dispute, but reasons that are considered adequate by thousands are objectively adequate. Otherwise, many actions would be objectively irrational that thousands of people would advocate to others that they do. Thus, for them "objectively irrational" would no longer be the fundamental normative concept.

15. The present account of objectively irrational actions and personally irrational actions and of the distinction between them is the result of continuing criticisms of earlier accounts by my son, Joshua. However, he probably has further criticisms of the present account. For his account of rationality, see *Brute Rationality* (Cambridge: Cambridge University Press, 2004).

16. One factor that made it difficult for me, and for other philosophers as well, to provide an adequate account of irrationality and rationality and their relationship to reasons is that the ordinary sense of "irrational" and "rational" applied to actions, beliefs, and desires is the personal sense, and the ordinary sense of "a reason" is the objective sense. This makes it very tempting to distort the sense of either "irrational" and "rational" or "a reason." In earlier works, I succumbed to the latter temptation.

17. The phrases "justifying force" and "requiring force" are derived from Joshua Gert. The use of "force" rather than "strength" was suggested by Ted Bond and endorsed by Esther Gert.

18. Certain socially sanctioned desires, such as the desire to climb mountains, to satisfy which many people are prepared to suffer considerable harms, do seem to provide basic reasons. However, this is because a significant number of people believe this kind of action will have sufficiently good consequences to be an adequate reason for suffering the harms. This common knowledge accounts for the fact that even though a person may have no conscious belief that satisfying his desire to climb a mountain will have these consequences, we do not count his suffering of harms in order to satisfy his desire as personally irrational, that is, as counting in favor of his having a mental disorder. However, if a person has a desire such that satisfying it significantly increases his risk of suffering a nontrivial harm and if acting on that desire is not regarded by a significant number of people as having consequences that provide an adequate reason for satisfying it, then having that desire is regarded as a mental disorder and acting to satisfy it is a symptom of that disorder.

19. Three examples are Henry Sidgwick, Kurt Baier, and Thomas Nagel.

20. He remains impartial even if, completely unknown to him, one team happens to get the wider strike zone more often than the other. That this can happen is why consistency as well as impartiality is required for a good umpire.

21. This definition of impartiality, properly interpreted, is adequate for the standard kind of impartiality, that required of referees, umpires, and judges, where the person who is required to be impartial is not in the group with regard to which he is required to be impartial. The proper interpretation allows for a person to apply a rule impartially even when the rule specifies that people with particular features are benefited or harmed more than people with other features, e.g., giving more benefits to those who are more productive. "Benefit" and "harm" also have to be understood as referring not only to basic harms and benefits but also to what are regarded as benefits and harms in the context of the activity or game, e.g., winning is a benefit and losing is a harm.

However, even with this interpretation, the definition is not adequate for the impartiality required when the person who is required to be impartial is a member of the group with regard to which he is required to be impartial, which is the case with the impartiality required by morality. Morality not only requires not being influenced by the particular persons who will be harmed or benefited by one's impartial following of the rule, it also requires that one make no special exceptions with regard to who is allowed to violate a rule. The definition of standard impartiality provided does not capture this aspect of the impartiality that is required by morality. Rather, this aspect of impartiality includes what Kant attempted to capture, but did not, by claiming that morality required one to act only on maxims that one could will to be universal laws or universal laws of nature. Moral impartiality not only requires impartiality with regard to who in the group is benefited or harmed but also requires that one make no special exceptions for oneself or friends with regard to who can violate the moral rule in the same morally relevant circumstances. See B. Gert, *Morality: Its Nature and Justification*, rev. ed. (New York: Oxford University Press, 2005), 214–216.

22. Former moral agents who are still conscious would also be included in this impartially protected group.

23. Mill makes the same point about impartiality. See *Utilitarianism*, chap. 5, par. 9.

24. Kant claims that the function of the faculty of reason must be to do that which it can do better than any other faculty, such as instinct. He couples this with the additional claim that instinct would serve better than reason to make us happy and so concludes that if reason has a practical function it must be something other than prudential. Kant claims that reason provides the Categorical Imperative: Act only on that maxim that you can will to be a universal law. Given his intellectualist account of reason, Kant requires that actions in violation of the Categorical Imperative involve contradictions or other kinds of impossibilities or inconsistencies.

25. See "Le Droit de Nature," in *Le Pouvoir et le Droit: Hobbes et les fondements de la loi,* compiled by Louis Roux and François Tricaud (Saint-Étienne: Publications de l'Université de Saint-Étienne, 1992), 27–48.

26. This is true except in the trivial sense that all rational persons could publicly allow never following any moral ideal.

27. Mill, *Utilitarianism*, chap. 5, par. 9.

28. G. E. Moore claimed that beauty, even if it would never be experienced by any sentient being, had intrinsic value, but he did not discuss whether it was rational to suffer any harm to protect a beautiful environment that would never be experienced by anyone.

29. This would be a form of act consequentialism.

30. See note 13, part I.

31. See *Leviathan*, chap. 11, par. 21.

‼ Index

Abilities
  loss of, 33–34, 91 (*see also* Disability)
  mental, 34
  of moral agents, 87
  physical, 34
  volitional, 34, 156n. 14 (*see also*
    Volitional disability)
Abortion, 6
  dispute about, 126
  laws concerning, 138–39
  as morally controversial, 6, 126, 139
  as related to scope of morality, 14,
    126
  an unresolvable question, 14, 130–31
Acceptability
  of alternative views, 147
  moral, xvi, 19–20
Actions
  alternative, 69–70
  altruistic, 115
  appraising, 97–98, 99–100
  done freely, 70
  done intentionally, 70–71
  done knowingly, 70–71
  free, 156n. 14
  of governments, 56
  intentional, 156n. 14
  irrational (*see* Irrational actions)

kind of, 9
  moral judgments about, 10–11
  rational (*see* Rational actions)
  rationally required, 98
  same kind of, 15, 20, 58–74, 123
  voluntary, 156n. 14
Activity
  criminal, 67, 121, 134
  voluntary, 45, 49
Addictions, 34
Adequate evidence, 63
Adequate justification, 5, 9–10, 24, 47
  legal versus moral, 48–49
Adequate reasons, 12, 88, 112–14
  objectively, 97, 101
  personally, 100–101
Adequately informed, 24
Agreement, widespread, 8–10
  about morality, 5
Alternative actions, 13, 156n. 16
Alternatives
  as morally relevant feature, 69–70
  to physician assisted suicide, 69–70
  rational, 98
Altruistic actions, 115
American Psychiatric Association,
    159n. 11
Anger, 31, 99, 102. *See also* Displeasure

Animals
    not moral agents, 10–11, 33, 143
    treatment of controversial, 6, 14,
        28–29, 118, 128–29, 141, 146
Annoyance, 144. *See also* Displeasure
Anthropologists, xv
Anxiety, 31, 72
Applied ethics, vii, 15
Aristotle, 85
Arrogance, 135. *See also* Humility
Attitude
    toward moral disagreement, 146
    toward morality, 83–84
Audi, Robert, xii–xiii
Austin, J. L., 156n. 15, 159n. 10

"Bad," "good," "ought," "right,"
    and "wrong," 11
Baier, Kurt, ix, xiv, 161n. 19
Baron, Marcia, xiv
Baseball umpire, 117, 121
Baum, Robert, xvii
Beliefs
    accepted by all moral agents, 83,
        88–90, 154n. 4
    conscious, 160–61n. 18
    false, 41, 96
    in God, 132
    irrational (*see* Irrational beliefs)
    as morally relevant feature, 63–64
    as motives, 104–5
    non-motivating, 100–101
    personal, 158n. 3
    as personal reasons for acting,
        100–101, 104–5, 108, 160n. 16
    rational, 105
    rationally required, 83–85, 88–91,
        125, 127, 158–59nn. 3, 4, 6

    relevant, 63–64
    religious, 4, 17, 30, 83, 128, 129,
        154n. 4
    scientific, 83, 90, 128
Benefits. *See* Goods
Bentham, Jeremy, 28, 60, 66, 127
Berger, Edward M., xiv–xv
"Bernard Gert's *Morality* and its
        application to computer ethics"
        (Triplett), 157–58n. 28
Bernat, James L., xv, 157n. 24
Bioethics: A Return to Fundamentals
    (Gert, Culver, Clouser), xvii, 157nn.
        24, 27
Blamed, 32, 43
"blamed than applauded," 127
Blindfold of justice, 83
    and impartiality, 90–91, 119
    versus veil of ignorance, 90, 91, 119
Blinding a person, 33
Blindness, desiring, 112
Bond, Edward J., xiii, xvi, 160n. 17
Boraz, Edward, xvii
Borchert, Donald, xvii
Brandt, Richard, 159n. 12
Brock, Dan, xiii, 155n. 5
Bumping into, 38

Callousness, 76–77, 133
Cancer, 98, 101
Carson, Thomas, xiv
Categorical Imperative, vii, 57, 119–21,
    123. *See also* Kant
Celebrity, 144
Chang, Ruth, xiv
Character, 135
    moral, 26, 54
Character traits. *See* Virtues and vices

Cheating (Do not cheat), 9, 20, 27,
    44–46, 56–57, 134
  and breaking promises, 44
  and deceiving, 45
  and fairness, 46
  and games, 45–46
  justified, 46
  paradigm of, 44
  similarities to breaking a law, 49
  at solitaire, 44–45
Children, 11, 26–27, 118–19
  bringing up, 136
  father's relation to, 116–17
  intelligence of, 87
  learning to make moral decisions, 76
  mother's relation to, 10
  my, xvii
  parents' relation to, 65, 115–16, 128, 136
  protected by common morality, 28,
    128, 130
  saving, 24
Chimpanzees, 10, 14, 28, 118
Circumcision, female, 39
Circumstances, same, 123
Citizens, 65, 90, 140
Civil disobedience, 54, 57, 139
Clouser, K. Danner, xvii, 157nn. 24, 27
Coercion, 35, 70
Cohen, Eunice and Julian, xi–xii
Common Morality, v–viii, 6–12, 84,
    125. See also Morality
  justification of, 81–86
"Common Morality and Computers"
    (Gert), 157–58n. 28
Competence, 64
Compulsion, 34
Computer, xv, 148–49, 157–58n. 28
  crimes, 134

Concert, 36, 39
Condemnation, 98
Conscience, 142
Consciousness, 127, 130
  increase of, 104
  permanent loss of, 30
    (see also Death)
  temporary loss of, 30
Consent, 38, 73, 75
  valid, 35, 64, 143
Consequences, 60–61, 141. See also
    Evils; Goods
  actual, 61
  of alternative laws, 75
  of alternative policies, 69
  beneficial (see Goods)
  different estimates of, 15
  direct and indirect, 56
  emotional and financial, 57
  estimating, 74–76
  of everyone knowing, 19, 74–76
  foreseeable, 61–62
  foreseen, 61–62
  harmful (see Evils)
  intended, 61–62
  legitimately ignorant of, 11, 27
  of morality not providing unique
    answers, 145–47
  as a morally relevant feature,
    60–62
  overall, 56
  of particular actions, 56–57
  probability of, 13
  of being publicly allowed, 74–76
  ranking, 79
  short-term, 87
  unforeseeable, 61
  unknowable, 11

Consequentialism, 154n. 1
  act, 156n. 16, 156–57n. 20,
    161–62n. 28
  negative, 156n. 16
  rule, 156–57n. 20
Consistency and impartiality, 117, 121,
    161n. 20
Contracts, 42, 142. *See also* Promises
Copp, David, xiii
Country, 85, 90
Courage as personal virtue, 77
Cowardice as personal vice, 77
Criminal
  activity, 67, 121, 134
  law, 35–36
Criterian, 31
"Criterian and Human Nature" (Gert),
    155n. 9
Cruelty, 76
  to animals, 141
Culver, Charles M., xvii, 157nn. 24, 27

Dartmouth College, xi, xiv–xv
Darwin, Charles, 155n. 10
De Cive (Hobbes), 157n. 23
Death, x, 7, 12, 91, 114. *See also* Killing
  and permanent loss of
    consciousness, 30
Deceitfulness, 77
Deceiving (Do not deceive), 6, 9, 15,
    20, 29–30, 40–42, 51, 74, 89
  animals, 29
  and cheating, 44
  paternalistic, 69
  and personal appearance, 41
Decision
  government, 140–42, 148
  impartial, 50

making bodies, 147
  moral, v, vi, 3, 6, 16–17
  procedure, viii, 148
  rational, 64
  split, 120
Deigh, John, xiii
Democracy, 147
Deontology, 156n. 19
  and rule consequentialism,
    156–57n. 20
Dependability, 77
Depriving (*see also* Causing an evil)
  of ability, 33–34
  of freedom, 9, 10, 35–38, 39
  of opportunity, 36–37
  of pleasure, 9, 38–39
  what counts as, 36–37
Desires
  to avoid harm, 89
  irrational, 112
  maximizing satisfaction of, 95–96
  as morally relevant feature, 62–63
  not basic reasons, 111–12
  overpowering, 100, 101
  rational, 62–63
  rationally required, 89
  and reasons, 111–12
*Diagnostic and Statistical Manual of
    Mental Disorders, Fourth Edition*
    (DSM IV), 159n. 11
Disability (Do not disable), 30, 33–35
  and Do not deprive of freedom,
    33–34
  mental, 33–34
  physical, 33–34
  and temporary loss of consciousness,
    30
  volitional, 34, 88

Disagreement, viii, 13–15
    allowed by common morality, 28, 84
    factual, 13–14
    ideological, 15
    among impartial rational persons,
        51, 57
    about interpretation of moral
        rules, 15
    moral, x, 5–6, 13–15, 20, 139–42
    occur within an area of agreement,
        vi, x, 12, 138
    political, 15
    in ranking evils (harms), 12, 14–15, 20
    religious, 140
    about scope of morality, 14, 28–29,
        126–30, 140, 146
    sources of, 14–15
    unresolvable, 6, 14, 20, 29, 138
Disease. See Malady
Dishonesty, 77
Disobedience. See Civil disobedience;
    Violation of moral rules
Disorder, mental, 96, 101
Displeasure, 31, 40
    and failing to satisfy a desire, 111
Distribution, 60, 66
Doctors. See Physicians
Doctrine of double effect, 71, 157n. 26
Dolphins, 11, 14, 28, 118
Driver, Julia, xiv
"Le Droit de Nature" (Gert), 161n. 24
Duggan, Timothy J., xii, 156n. 14
Duties (Do your duty), xiii, 20,
        50–53, 54
    can arise from circumstances, 51–52
    arise from jobs and positions, 51, 53
    of doctors, 40–41
    of governments, 145

of imperfect obligation, 52, 156n. 17
can never require acting immorally,
        50–51
not the same as moral requirements, 53
of perfect obligation, 52, 156n. 18

Education, right to, 145
Egoistic, 102
Emergency as a morally relevant
        feature, 72–73
Emotional involvement, 16
Emotions, 16, 155n. 11. See also Feelings
    strong, 99, 101
Enforcement, 67–68. See also
        Punishment
Environment, 128
Envy, 155n. 11
Ethical Issues in Neurology (Bernat), xv
Ethical relativism, 5
Ethics
    anthropology code of, xv
    applied and professional, 15
    business, xv
    computer, xv
    courses, vii, xvii
    medical, xv
Ethics committees, 13, 147
Euthanasia, 35
Evils (harms), 21, 97
    agreement about basic, 12
    to animals and plants, 28–29
    caused by infants or animals, 33
    caused by religion, 115
    and deprivation of goods, 67
    disagreement in ranking, 12, 14–15,
        20, 60, 91, 140, 146, 159n. 5
    estimating, 7
    false beliefs as, 41

Evils (harms) (*continued*)
  not a homogenous category, 21
  all humans can suffer, 12
  list of, 6, 40, 84,
  and maladies, 40
  and moral ideals, 7, 22–26
  and moral rules, 7, 12, 21–22, 23
  as morally relevant feature, 60–61
  to oneself, 108
  to others 109
  preventing, 51–52
  and punishment, 40, 53–54, 68–69
  all rational persons want to avoid,
    7, 12
  and reasons, 103–4
  risk of, 13
Exceptions for self and friends,
    121, 123
Excuses
  complete, 33, 70, 88
  partial, 33, 70
  "A Plea for Excuses," 159n. 10
  versus justifications, 43–44, 70
Exemplify, 78
*Expression of the Emotions in Man and
  Animals, The* (Darwin), 155n. 10
Expressions as criterian of feelings, 31

Facts
  agreement on, 17
  disagreement about, 13, 139–40
  about human nature, 12–13
  known by all moral agents, 88–90
  morally relevant, 58–73
  as objective reasons, 104
  provided to computer, 148–49
  social, 89–90
  that can justify, 104, 108

  that can make actions irrational,
    106, 108
  universal, 12–13
  versus beliefs, xiii, 103–4
Fairness and cheating, 46, 77
Fallibility
  feature of human nature, 8, 13, 84,
    88–89, 148
  and humility, 135
Family, 6, 132
Fanatic, religious, 127
Features
  of an adequate justification, 9–10
  of common morality, viii–ix, 7–8
  of human nature, v, 7–8
  of moral judgments, 10–11
  of moral system, 16–17
  morally relevant, 10
Feelings
  criterian of, 31
  hurting, 15
  unpleasant, 31–32, 39, 155n. 11
Female circumcision, 39
Fetus, 14, 28, 71, 118, 128–30, 138–39,
    155n. 8
Finger, 107
Flourishing, 26
Fluehr-Lobban, Carolyn, xv
Food and fluids, 69–70
Foreseeable consequences, 61–62
Foreseen consequences, 61–62
Fortitude, 78
Fractions of a cent, 134
Frank H. Kenan Fellowship, xii
"Free Will as the Ability to Will"
  (Gert), 156n. 14
Freedom (Do not deprive of freedom),
    35–38

and Do not disable, 33–34
Friends, 6, 13, 123, 132
Fully protected, 28
Fully responsible, 89, 153n. 3

Games, 44–45, 137–38
    and cheating, 44–45
    unfair, 46
Gender, 155n. 8
Gert
    Bernard, xii–xiii, 156n. 14, 157–58nn.
        24, 27, 28
    Esther, xvii, 160n. 17
    Heather, xvii, 151, 152, 156n. 13
    Joshua, xiii, xviii, 160nn. 15, 17
God, 132, 133, 158n. 3. *See also*
    Religion
God's eye point of view, 116
Golden Rule, The, vii
Golf, 44
Goods (benefits)
    depriving of, 67
    as morally relevant feature, 66–67
    promoting, xiii, 24
    rankings of, 12–13, 14–15, 91, 140,
        146, 159n. 5
    and Utilitarian ideals, 81
Gossip, 32
Governments
    and Classical Utilitarianism, 66
    democratic, v
    policies, 75
    and positive rights, 145
    relationship to citizens, 65, 140
    and unresolvable moral
        disagreements, 139–42
    and violations of moral rules, 65
    versus individuals, 65–66

Grammar and morality, 7–8, 15–17
Gratitude, 78
Grounding for the Metaphysics of Morals
    (Kant), 154–55n. 4
Group
    dominant, 6, 83
    ethnic, national, racial, or religious,
        83, 118, 127, 132
    impartially protected, 126–31, 141
    minimal, 127–30
    presupposed by impartiality, 116–17,
        126
    significant, 113–14
    subordinate, 6, 83

Haksar, Vinit, xvii
Happiness, 136
Harms. *See* Evils
Health care, right to, 145
Hennessey, John, xv
Hitchcock Hospital, xv
Hobbes, Thomas, 7, 47, 69, 78, 85, 124,
    136, 140, 149
Honesty, 7
Hospital ethics committee, xv, 147
Human beings, ix, 12
Human Genome Project, xv
Human nature, v, 4, 8, 12–13, 15
Human rights, 142–43
Human well-being, 23
Humanly possible, 118
Humility, xviii, 135. *See also*
    Arrogance
Hybrid concept of rationality, 106
Hypocrisy, 6, 86

Impartial rational persons, 17
    can disagree, 5–6

Impartiality, v, xiv, 7, 10, 90, 116–19
   and Bentham, 127
   and blindfold of justice, 90, 119
   and Categorical Imperative, 57,
      119–21, 123
   common mischaracterizations of,
      116–17
   as complex concept, 121
   and consistency, 117, 121
   definition of, 117
   general, 116
   and God's eye point of view, 116
   and group, 126–31
   and Kant, viii, 119–21, 122, 123, 124,
      127
   mistaken descriptions of, 10, 116–117
   moral (see Moral impartiality)
   and moral ideals, 124
   and moral rules, 10, 122–25
   not a moral virtue, 121
   presupposes a respect and a group,
      116–18, 121
   and rationality, 116
   and Rawls, 90, 119–121
   related to morality, 33
   required by morality, viii, 10, 118
   and treating like cases alike, 117
   of an umpire, 117
   and unanimity, 119–20
   and veil of ignorance, 90, 119–20
Imprudence, 77
Infants. See Children
Informal public system, morality as an,
      137–39
   presupposes overwhelming
      agreement, 137
Insights, 82, 153n. 2
Integrity, moral, 147

Intemperance, 77
Intention, statement of, 42
Intentional
   actions, 38
   violation, 21, 36
Intentionally
   acting, 21
   causing a harm, 31–32, 35
   touching, 38
   versus knowingly, 21, 70–71
Interpretation
   of a moral rule, 15, 20, 29–53, 140
   of a rule of baseball, 17
Irrational actions, 92–93, 97–103
   and desires, 112
   and immoral actions, 85–86, 131–33
   involves harm to the agent, 102, 106
   mistaken definition of, 95–96
   and morally required action, 131–32
   not to endorse morality, 83–84
   objectively, 97–99, 101
   otherwise, 104–5, 106–8
   personally, 99–103
Irrational beliefs, 63–64, 92–93, 105
Irrational desire, 63–64, 92–93
Irrational doubt, 89
Irrationality, 91–95. See also Rationality
   analysis of, 92
   as fundamental normative concept,
      86, 93–94
   and impartiality, 116
   more basic than rationality, xiv,
      91–103

Jainism, 28
Job and duties, 51
Journal of Value Inquiry, xiv
Judge, 50. See also Referee; Umpire

Judgments
  legal, 8
  moral (*see* Moral judgments)
  religious, 8
  of responsibility, 70
Judicial decision, 140
Justification, 19. *See also* Moral
      justification
  adequate, 9–10, 47
  and excuse, 43–44
  legal versus moral, 48–49
  of morality, ix, 3, 8
  needed for violations of moral
      rules, 9
  not needed for failing to follow
      moral ideals, 23
Justified following of moral ideals, 76
Justified violations
  strongly, 57
  weakly, 57
Justifying
  common morality, 38
  force of reasons, 106–11
  moral impartiality, 122–30
  reasons as, 106–11
  violations of moral rules, 16, 55–76

Kagan, Shelly, xiii
Kamm, Frances, xiv
Kant, Immanuel, vii, viii, 3, 7, 26, 28,
      43, 52, 56, 57, 82, 85, 86, 119–24,
      127, 154n. 4
Kettner, Matthias, xiii
Killing (Do not kill), 29–30
  animals, 28
  interpretations of, 30
  and permanent loss of consciousness,
      30

Kindness, 76
Knowingly
  versus intentionally, 21, 61, 70–71
  versus without knowledge, 70
Knowledge
  limited, 13, 88–89 (*see also* Fallibility)
  of moral rules, 91
  necessary to be moral agent, 74–76,
      77, 88–91

La Rochefoucauld, 86
Ladenson, Robert, xvii
Law (Obey the law), 47–49, 141–42
  and cheating, 49
  and conscience, 142
  criminal, 35–36
  definition of, 47–48
  enforcement, 67–68
  and freedom, 35–36
  good, 47
  immoral, 47
  and morality, 8, 137–38
  and morally unresolvable issues, 138
  Natural, ix
  and politics, 138
  prohibiting abortion, 138, 141
  and rights, 142–43
  strict liability, 48
  tax, 47, 49
  traffic, 47
"Le Droit de Nature" (Gert), 161n. 24
Legal judgment, versus moral
      judgment, 8
Legal rights, 142
Legal system, 47–49
  versus moral system, 48–49
Legalizing physician-assisted suicide,
      69–70

Le Pouvoir et le Droit: Hobbes et les fondements de la loi, 161n. 24
Leviathan (Hobbes), 156n. 15, 157n. 23, 162n. 30
Liability
    to punishment, 53–55
    strict, 48
Life
    loss of, 30 (*see also* Death)
    of mother versus life of fetus, 71
    prolonging operation, 63–64
    prolonging treatment, 98, 114
    saving a person's, 9, 107
Limited knowledge. *See* Fallibility
Lottery, punishment, 55, 157n. 22
Lottery winner, 25
Love
    and anger, 102
    of parents for children, 136
Luck, 11, 76
Lying (Do not lie), 15. *See also* Deceiving
    definition, 40
    promise, 43

MacLean, Doug, xiv
Malady and evils, 40
Maximizing satisfaction of desires view, 80–81
McNamara, Paul, xvi, 159n. 9
Medicine, goals of, 21
Mental disorder, 96, 100–101
Mill, John Stuart, vii, viii, 3, 7, 23, 26, 27, 28, 52, 56, 57, 66, 85, 124, 159n. 10, 161n. 22
Minimal group protected by morality, 127
Mogielnicki, R. P., 157n. 24

Moor, Jim, xiv
Moore, G. E., 161–62n. 27
Moral agent, 8–9, 26–27. *See also* Rational person
    beliefs of, 88–91
    characteristics of, 87–88
Moral attitude, 83
Moral decisions, v, vi, 4, 6, 9, 16–17
Moral disagreement
    due to rankings of goods and evils, 14–15
    ideological, 15
    some unresolvable, 6, 14
    sources of, 13–15, 140
Moral ideals, 7, 9, 22–26
    and callousness, 76–77
    encourages lessening harms, 7, 9, 20–26
    expresses point of morality, 26
    and impartiality, 25
    and imperfect duties, 26
    and kindness, 76
    and moral rules, xiii, 9
    and moral vice, 76–77
    and moral virtues, 76
    and morally good actions, 9
    and utilitarian ideals, 24–25
Moral impartiality, 118–31 (impartiality required by morality)
    and Bentham, 127
    and blindfold of justice, 119
    and Categorical Imperative, 119–21, 123
    disagreement about group toward which required, 126–31
    incompatible with arrogance, 135
    justifying, 122–31
    and Kant, 119–21, 124, 127

and moral ideals, 118, 124–25
must be humanly possible, 118
and publicly allowing, 122–23
and Rawls, 119–21
not required with respect to
    following moral ideals, 124
required with respect to obeying
    moral rules, 122–24
and two step procedure, 125
and unanimity, 119–20
and veil of ignorance, 119–20
with regard to group, 126–31
with respect to moral rules, 122–25
Moral issues
    are not all resolvable, vii
    controversial, v, viii, 12
Moral decisions, v, vi, 4, 6, 9, 16–17
Moral evaluation, xiv
Moral judgments, v, vi, 4, 6, 9, 16–17
    about people, 10,
    and Classical Utilitarianism, 66
    complete excuses rule out, 27
    distinguishing features, 10–11
    and Negative Utilitarianism, 66
    not about actions of people who
        cannot control actions, 27
    not for unforeseeable consequences,
        61
    only about actions of people who
        understand, 10–11
    only about actions of people not
        legitimately ignorant, 11, 27
    versus judgment of responsibility, 70
Moral matters, 8
Moral rights, 142–43
Moral rules, 7, 20–22. *See also particular
    rules*
    apply to, 26–27

first five, 21, 29, 40, 75
general characteristics of, 26–29
interpretations of, 29–53
justifying violations of, 55, 57–76
list of, 20
as morally relevant feature, 59–60
prohibit causing harm, 7
protect, 28–29
second five, 21, 29, 75
and Ten Commandments, 4
which violated as morally relevant
    feature, 59–60
*Moral Rules, The: A New Rational
    Foundation for Morality* (Gert), ix,
    xi, xii
Moral skepticism, 125
Moral system, 19–80 (*see also*
    Morality)
    features of, 19–20
    has practical value, xv
    as an informal public system,
        137–39
    and moral virtues, 76–77
    not derived from moral theory, v
    test of, 78–79
Moral theory, viii, 81–131
    complete, 148–49
    and Kant, vii, viii, 7
    and Hobbes, 7
    and Mill, vii, viii, 7
    my, xi
    should explain and justify both
        agreement and disagreement, viii
    standard, 7
Moral tolerance, 5
Moral virtues and vices, 76–78
    and children, 76
    and personal virtues, 77–78

Moral virtues and vices (*continued*)
  related to moral rules and ideals,
    76–78
  and social virtues, xiii, 78
Morality
  agreement about content, 5
  common (*see* Common morality)
  concerned with consequences, viii
  concerned with how people behave
    toward others, xiv
  and conscience, 142
  definition of, xiii
  descriptions of, v, vi, vii, 3
  does not settle controversial issues, v
  endorsed by all rational persons, vi
  and grammar, 7–8, 15–17
  and human nature, 3, 4,8
  includes two-step procedure for cases
    of conflict, 7
  and impartiality, 3
  incorrect view of, 6
  as an informal public system that
    applies to all, 137–39
  justification of, 81–87
  Kantian, 3
  and law, 8, 137–30
  more concerned with lessening of
    evil, viii
  must be acceptable to all rational
    persons, viii–ix
  must be known to all normal adults,
    ix, 3
  point of, 7
  as a public system, xiv, 8
  and rationality, v, vi, xiv, xvii, 3,
    114–16
  and religion, xiv, 4, 8
  requires impartiality, viii
    revised versions of, 3–4
    scope of, 14, 28–29, 126–30, 140, 146
    and self interest, 114–16
    understood by all moral agents, 8
    Utilitarian, 3–4
*Morality: A New Justification of the
    Moral Rules* (Gert), ix, xi
Morality: Its Nature and Justification
    (Gert), ix, xii, xiii, xiv, xvi
Morality and the New Genetics (Gert),
    xv, 4
"*Morality versus Slogans,*" 153n. 1
"Morally bad," "morally good,"
    "morally ought," "morally right,"
    and "morally wrong," 11
Morally relevant features, 58–74
  as answers to morally relevant
    questions, 59
  determine the kind of violation,
    58–59
  must be understood by all moral
    agents, 59, 74
  summary of, 73–74
  used in first step of two step
    procedure, 58
Morally relevant questions, list of,
    59–73
Morally wrong, 154n. 2
Mothers, 10
Motives
  are beliefs, 103
  as explanations of actions, 103–4
  versus reasons, 103–6
Music, 39

Nagel, Thomas, 161n. 19
National Endowment for the
    Humanities (NEH), xi

National Humanities Center, xii
National Science Foundation, xi
Nationalism, 115
Natural law, ix, 153n. 2, 157n. 23
Negative Consequentialism
    (Utilitarianism), viii, 156n. 16
Neonate, 141
Normative character of rationality and
    irrationality, 7, 86–87, 91–95, 96,
    110–11, 113, 115, 131, 159n. 10,
    160n. 14
Nurse, 71

Objective
    factors, 62
    rationality of an act, 113
    reasons, 103–4, 108, 111–12
    sense of "irrational," 97
    sense of rationality, xiii, 97
    sense of "a reason," 97
Objectively
    adequate reason, 97
    irrational action, 97–99, 101
    rational action, 113–14
Obligation
    duty of imperfect, 52, 156n. 17
    duty of perfect, 52, 156n. 18
Omissions. See also Actions
Opportunity, 36–37, 39. See also
    Freedom
Ownership, 35. See also Law

Pain (Do not cause pain), 31–33, 144
    including all unpleasant feelings, 31
    ranking, 21, 114
    rational persons seek to avoid, 7, 12
Parents, 65,115–16, 128, 136
Paternalism, 64, 69, 157n. 27

Patience, 78
"Patient Refusal of Hydration and
    Nutrition: An Alternative to
    Physician Assisted Suicide or
    Voluntary Euthanasia" (Bernat),
    157n. 24
Patients, terminally ill, 15
Personal appearance, 41
Personal guide, x
Personal reasons, 100–101, 104–6, 111
Personal sense of rationality, xiii
Personal virtues and vices, 77–78
Personally adequate reason, 100–101
Personally irrational action, 99–103
Philips, David, xiv
Philosophy and Phenomenological
    Review, xiii, xiv, 155n. 5
Phobia, 34
Physician assisted suicide, 69–70
Physicians, xv, 24, 64, 72, 98, 114
Plato, vi, 43, 114
Pleasure (Do not deprive of pleasure),
    xiv, 38–39
    account of, 38
    depriving of, 9, 12
    loss of, 7, 12
    preventing loss of pleasure, 9
    and satisfaction of desire, 111
Police, 23, 51, 67
Polite, 120
Political
    disagreements, 15
    institutions, v
    rights, 145
    situation, 66
    solution, 140
    theory, 85, 147
Praise, 11

Pregnant woman, 128–29, 139
Preventing violations as a morally
    relevant feature, 67–68
Prince, Gregory, xi
Principle of Utility, vii
Privacy, 38, 144
Procedures, 12
    decision, viii, 148
    morally acceptable, v
    simple, vi–vii
    two-step, 7, 58–76, 125, 143, 146
        (see also Two-step procedure)
Prohibitions, religious, 4
Promises (Keep your promises), 42–44
    breaking, 9
    and cheating, 44
    as a statement of intention, 42
Prudence, 77
Public system, xiv (see also Moral system)
    morality as a, 137–39
Punishment
    and evils, 40
    and God, 132
    liability to, 53–55
    lottery, 55, 157n. 22
    as a morally relevant feature, 68
    publicly allowed, 152
    versus revenge, 68

Qualified person, 36, 57, 158n. 3

Race, 36, 85, 118, 127, 155n. 8, 158n. 3
Racist, 118, 127
Rankings of goods and evils, 12–13,
    14–15, 91, 140, 146, 159n. 5
Rational actions (see also Irrational
        actions)
    based on best reasons, 109–10
    as maximizing satisfaction of desires,
        95–96
    as not irrational, 94–95
Rational alternatives, 98
Rationality, xiii, xvii, 91–95 (see also
        Irrationality)
    analysis of, 92–93
    as fundamental normative concept,
        86–87, 91–95, 96, 110–11, 113, 115,
        131, 159n. 10, 160n. 14
    and human nature, v, 8, 12–13
    as a hybrid concept, 106
    and impartiality, 92
    and irrationality, xiv, 91–95
    and Kant, 86
    and morality, vi, 114–16
    objective, xiii, 97–99
    personal, xiii, 99–103
    and Rawls, 120
    and self-interest, 114–16
*Rationality, Rules, and Ideals: Critical
        Essays on Bernard Gert's Moral
        Theory*, xii–xiii
Rationally acceptable, 17
Rationally allowed, 6
    actions, 98
Rationally required, 111
    actions, 98
    beliefs, 83–85, 88–91, 125, 127, 129,
        152, 158–59nn. 3, 4, 6
    desires, 84
Rawls, John, 90, 119–20, 153n. 2,
    159n. 8
Reasons, 103
    for acting immorally, 134–35
    for acting morally, 134–35
    adequate, 12, 112–14
    basic, 133

best, 109–10
better or stronger, 107–8
and desires 111–12
direct and indirect, 134–36
as facts, xiii, 103–4
and interests of others, 109
justifying force of, 106–11
motivating, 105
non-motivating, 101
objective sense, 103–4
personal sense, 100–101, 104–6
as rational beliefs, 104–5
requiring force of, 109–10
of self interest, 109–10, 133
versus motives, 103–6
Referee, 120. *See also* Judge;
    Umpire
Refusal
of food and fluids, 157n. 24
of treatment, 7
Relationship between victim and
    violator as morally relevant
    feature, 65–66
Relativism, ethical, 5. *See also* Ethical
    relativism
Religion, 36, 85, 118, 127, 158n. 3
    (*see also* God)
and morality, 4
Religious
beliefs, 4, 17, 30, 83, 129, 154n. 4
considerations, 141
disagreement, 140
fanatics, 127
group, 83, 86, 132
guide, x
judgments, 8
slogans, vii
support, 4

texts, 3
traditions, 5
views, x,
Reporter/photographer, 144
Republic, The (Plato), 43
Requiring force of reasons,
    109–10
Resources, 145
Respectful discussion, vi, 147
Responsibility judgments, 70
Revenge, 102
versus punishment, 66, 68
Ridge, Michael, xvii
Rights, 33, 142–45
negative, 144
positive, 145
"Rights and Rights Violators: A New
    Approach to the Nature of
    Rights" (Gert), 156n. 13
Rous, Louis, 161n. 24

Sabbath, 4
Sadness, 31
Samuels, Sheldon W., xvi
Satisfaction of desires, maximizing,
    95–96
Sayre-McCord, Geoffrey, xiii
Scope
of morality, 14, 28–29, 126–30, 140,
    146
of right to privacy, 144
Secrets, 51
Self interest
and morality, 114–16
and rationality, 114–16
and reasons, 9
Sentient beings, 128, 157–58n. 27
Sexist, 118, 127

Sexual pleasure, 39
Shame, 155n. 11
Sidgwick, Henry, 161n. 19
Sinnott Armstrong, Walter, ix, xii, xiii
Skepticism
  moral, 125
  philosophical, 90
Slogans, vii
Smith, Michael, xiii
Social contract theory, viii–ix,
Social virtues, xiii, 78
Society, 5, 47–50, 144–45
  decent, 136
  and morality, 26
  stability of, 49
Sociologists, 67
Solitaire, 44
Sources of moral disagreement, 140
Speaker, competent, 6
Stealing 37
Sterba, James, xiv
Stern, Larry, xii
Suffering. See Evils; Pain
Supreme Court, United States, 120

Tactless, 77
Tax laws, 47, 55
Teacher, 32, 46, 50, 117
Temperance, 77
Ten Commandments, The, vii, 4
Test of moral system, 78–79
Thayer School of Engineering, xi
Theory of Justice, A (Rawls), 90, 153n. 2, 159n. 8
Tickets, 36
Tolerance, moral, 5

Traits of character, 76, 78
Treatment, refusal of, 7
Tricaud, François, 161n. 24
Triplett, Timm, xvi, 157–58n. 28
Trust, 21–22, 90
  loss of, 29, 75
Truth (Tell the truth), 40, 77
Truthful, 77
Tuck School of Business, xi
Tugendhat, Ernst, xiii, 158–59n. 4
Two-step procedure, 7, 58–76, 125
  first step, 58–74
  second step, 74–76

Umpire, 117, 161n. 20. *See also* Judge; Referee
Unanimity, 119–20
Undependability, 77
Unfair, 46
Unfairness, 77
Unforeseeable consequences, 55, 61, 157n. 22
Unique answers, v, vi, vii, viii, 4, 48, 84, 125, 137–38, 145–48
Unique or close to unique position, 51–53
United States Supreme Court, 120
Unpleasant feelings, 31–32, 39, 155n. 11. *See also* Pain
Utilitarian ideals, 81
  and moral ideals, 24–25
  and social virtues, 8
Utilitarianism. *See also* Consequentialism
  classical, 66
  negative, 66
Utilitarianism (Mill), vii, 159n. 10, 161nn. 23, 27

Values, 13. *See also* Evils; Goods
Veil of ignorance, 119–21
  and blindfold of justice, 90
Violations of moral rules, 9–10
  intentional versus knowing as
    morally relevant feature,
    70–71,
  justifying, 55–76
  and liability to punishment, 53–55,
    57
  morally relevant features of,
    58–73
  need adequate justification,
    15–16
  and punishment, 68–69
  same kind of, 7
  strongly justified, 57
  and two-step procedure, 19
  unjustified, 57, 67–69
  weakly justified, 57, 67–69
  what counts as, 20–21

Virtues and vices
  moral, xiii, 76–78 (*see also* Moral
    virtues)
  personal, 77–78 (*see also* Personal
    virtues)
  social, xiii, 78
Volitional abilities and disabilities, 34,
  88, 156n. 14
Voluntary actions, 156n. 14
Voluntary activity, 44–45, 49
Vulnerability, v, 8, 12, 13, 84, 88, 148

Walk, taking a, 108, 111
Wart, 107
Why act morally, 131–36
Wincing, 31
Wittgenstein, 155n. 9
Wolf, Susan, xiii
Wolosin, Ilene, xvii

Yarnell, Patrick, xiv